Adam Davy's 5 Dreams about Edward II.

The Life of St. Alexius.

Solomon's Book of Wisdom.

St. Jeremie's 15 Tokens before Doomsday.

The Lamentacion of Souls.

BERLIN: ASHER & CO., 53 MOHRENSTRASSE.
NEW YORK: C. SCRIBNER & CO.; LEYPOLDT & HOLT.
PHILADELPHIA: J. B. LIPPINCOTT & CO.

Adam Davy's 5 Dreams about Edward II.

The Life of St. Alexius.

Solomon's Book of Wisdom.

St. Jeremie's 15 Tokens before Doomsday.

The Lamentacion of Souls.

EDITED
FROM THE LAUD MS. 622 IN THE BODLEIAN LIBRARY
BY
F. J. FURNIVALL, M.A.,
TRINITY HALL, CAMBRIDGE.

LONDON:
PUBLISHED FOR THE EARLY ENGLISH TEXT SOCIETY,
BY N. TRÜBNER & CO., 57 & 59, LUDGATE HILL.

Great Clarendon Street, Oxford OX2 6DP
United Kingdom

Oxford University Press is a department of the University of Oxford.
It furthers the University's objective of excellence in research, scholarship,
and education by publishing worldwide. Oxford is a registered trade mark of
Oxford University Press in the UK and in certain other countries

© The Early English Text Society 1873

The moral rights of the authors have been asserted

Database right Oxford University Press (maker)

First Edition published in 1873

All rights reserved. No part of this publication may be reproduced,
stored in a retrieval system, or transmitted, in any form or by any means,
without the prior permission in writing of Oxford University Press,
or as expressly permitted by law, or under terms agreed with the appropriate
reprographics rights organization. Enquiries concerning reproduction
outside the scope of the above should be sent to the Rights Department,
Oxford University Press, at the address above

You must not circulate this book in any other form
and you must impose this same condition on any acquirer

Published in the United States of America by Oxford University Press
198 Madison Avenue, New York, NY 10016, United States of America

British Library Cataloguing in Publication Data
Data available

Library of Congress Cataloging in Publication Data
Data available

Original Series, 69

ISBN 978-0-85-991837-4

CONTENTS.

	PAGE
FOREWORDS	7
ADAM DAVY'S 5 DREAMS ABOUT EDWARD II.	9
THE LEGEND OR LIFE OF ST. ALEXIUS, IN FOUR VERSIONS, FROM SIX MSS.	17
KING SOLOMON'S BOOK OF WISDOM. (A BOOK OF MORAL PRECEPTS AND PRACTICAL ADVICE)	81
ST. JEREMIE'S (JEROME'S) 15 TOKENS BEFORE DOOMSDAY, WITH LAMENTACIO ANIMARUM, AND A SONG ON THE COMING OF THAT SWEET DEW, CHRIST	91
SOLOMON'S CORONATION, DEEDS, AND JUDGMENT ON THE TWO MOTHERS' CLAIM TO ONE CHILD. HIS COURT AND TEMPLE	96
NOTES	99
INDEX	101

FOREWORDS.

ON the authority of Warton and Ritson, all the Poems in the Laud MS. 622 had been attributed to Adam Davy, the Marshal, of Stratford-at-Bow. My friend Professor Bernhard ten Brink of Strassburg, who is writing a History of English Literature, askt me the other day to examine the MS., and see what reason there was for supposing the whole volume to be by Davy. Last Wednesday, Nov. 25, 1875, before one of my 'Lectures to Ladies', at Oxford, 'on Anglo-Saxon and Early English Literature before Chaucer', I lookt through the Laud MS., and found no other reason for supposing Davy to be the author of all the poems (and prose Pilgrimage) in it, than the facts that the 72 leaves of it are in one scribe's handwriting, somewhat before 1400, and that on part of leaves 26 and 27 are Adam Davy's Dreams about King Edward the Second (1307-27), as I suppose, from his being calld specially 'Prince of Wales', l. 6. The last four pieces in the MS. are misplac't; they should be at the beginning. At present I see no reason why they, or the rest of the volume—except the short *Dreams*—should be assignd to Davy.

The Manuscript, Laud 622, is a large folio vellum one, double-columnd, roughly written in an unclerklike hand, seemingly before 1400,—1380-1400, says Mr Macray. It contains 9 sheets, *a* to *i* in eights: the first 8 leaves, *a* 1-8, come last. It begins, leaf 1 (= 9) with (1) 'þe Bataile of Ierusalem', generally call'd 'Siege of Jerusalem', whose head is on the last two leaves.

    And at þe fourty dayes ende
    Whider I wolde he bad me wende,
and ends on leaf 21, back, col. 1,
    God graunte vs alle þere to be
    Amen Amen par charite
  Here endeþ þe vengeaunce of goddes deth

Next follows, on leaf 21, back, col. 1, to leaf 26, back, col. 2, (2) 'The life of St Alexius' in 6-line stanzas, printed below.

Then comes (3) leaf 26, back, col. 2, to leaf 27, back, col. 1, l. 7, 'Adam Davy's Dreams'. This is followd by (4) leaf 27, back, col. 1, 'The Geste of Alisaunder', printed from this MS. in Weber's *Romances*, vol. i.

Diuers is þis mydellerede &c.—

This ends on leaf 64, col. 1, with "God vs graunte his blissyng'. Amen." Then comes (5) "þese arn þe pylgrimages of þe holy lond" (nearly 3 columns of prose); and then (6) the leaves which should come first: leaf 65, a long-line (2 in 1), ryming Bible History of Joseph (in Egypt, &c.), incomplete at the beginning; Moses and the golden calf, &c. &c., Solomon; with (leaf 70, back) "Elye. Eliseus. Danyel. Abacuk." Then (7) "Fiftene toknes Jeremie"; (8) Lamentacio animarum; (9) "þe Bataile of Ierusalem", which breaks off at leaf 72, back, with the catchwords, 'And atte fourty dayes ende', and which commences the volume in these words (see p. 9 here), 'And at þe fourty dayes ende'. Page 72, back, is in long lines (2 in 1): 'Listneþ alle þat beþ a-lyue! boþe cristen Men & wyue'; page 1 (the continuation) in short lines.

As Adam Davy has always been down in our lists for printing, I askt Mr George Parker to copy the old Marshal's *Dreams*, so that we might get done with him. The 'Life of Alexius', Solomon's 'Book of Wisdom', the well-known 'Fiftene Tokenes' in a fresh version, and the 'Lamentation of Souls', are added, just to make the Text thick enough to stand alone. The 'Pilgrimages of the Holy Land' I keep back for my volume on the subject, which has been long waiting for money to enable it to go to the printer.

The *Lamentacio Animarum* is a head-line in the MS. to the Continuation of the last of St. Jerome's *Fiftene toknes* before Doomsday, which Continuation describes the last Doom, and is followd by a pretty Song of Joy and Bliss for Christ's Coming. The Laud *Alexius* is a pathetically-told story. The other versions—added for comparison' sake—have less poetic merit.

3, St. George's Square, Primrose Hill, N.W.
Nov. 27, 1874.

Adam Daby's 5 Dreams about Edward II.

ADAM DAVY'S FIVE DREAMS ABOUT EDWARD II.

[*Laud MS.* 622 (*end of the* 14*th cent.*), *leaf* 26, *back.*]

<table>
<tr><td>

TO oure lorde Iesu crist in heuene,
Ich to-day shewe myne sweuene,
þat ich mette in one niȝth,
Of a kniȝth of mychel miȝth :   4
His name is ihote sir Edward þe kyng,
Prince of Wales[1], Engelonde þe faire þing.
Me mette þat he was armed wel,
Boþe wiþ yrne & wiþ stel ;   8
And on his helme þat was of stel,
A Coroune of gold bicom hym wel.
Bifore the shryne of seint Edward he stood,
Myd glad chere, & mylde of mood,   12
Mid two kniȝttes armed on eiþer side,
þat he ne miȝth þennes goo ne ride.
hetilich[2] hij leiden hym vpon,
Als hij miȝtten myd swerd don.   16
He stood þere wel swiþe stille,
And þoled al-to-gedres her wille ;

</td><td>

I dreamt one night

of King Edward,
Prince of Wales.
The First Dream.

That he stood, armd and crownd

before Saint Edward's Shrine.

Two knights

laid on him fiercely with their swords.

</td></tr>
</table>

[1] Compare "Nou is *Edward of Carnarvon*
        King of Engelond al aplyht",
in "The Elegy on the Death of Edw. I", from Harl. 2253, leaf 73, in Mr Thos. Wright's *Political Songs*, for the Camden Society, 1839, p. 249. Edw. III was never created Prince of Wales. The Black Prince was, but was never king.

[2] A.S. *hetelice*, hatefully, hotly.

1. ADAM DAVY'S 5 DREAMS ABOUT EDWARD II.

The King returnd no stroke,
No strook᷎ ne ȝaf he aȝeinward᷎
To þilk᷎ þat hym weren wiþerward᷎[1]. 20
but was not wounded.
Wounde ne was þere blody non,
Of al þat hym þere was don.
¶ After þat me þouȝth, onon,
When the 2 knights were gone,
As þe tweie kniȝttes weren gon, 24
In eiþer ere of oure kyng᷎
þere spronge out a wel fare þing᷎ :
Hij wexen out᷎ so briȝth so glem
four bright streams of different-coloured light
þat shyneþ of þe sonne-bem ; 28
Of diuers coloures hij weren,
flowd out of each of the King's ears.
þat comen out of boþe his eren
ffoure bendes alle by rewe on eiþer ere,
Of diuers colours, red᷎ & white als hij were ; 32
[leaf 27]
Als fer as me þou[ȝth] ich miȝth see,
hij spredden fer & wyde in þe cuntre.
fforsoþe me mette þis ilk᷎ sweuene—
This 1st Dream I dreamt on the Wednesday before Aug. 29, more than a year ago.
Ich take to witnesse god of heuene— 36
þe.wedenysday bifore þe decollacioun of seint Ion[2],
It is more þan twelue moneþ gon.
God me graunte so heuene blis,
As me mette þis sweuene as it is. 40
Now god þat is heuene kyng᷎,
To mychel ioye tourne þis metyng᷎ !

The Second Dream.
Noþer sweuene me mette, on a tiwes-niȝth 43
Bifore þe fest᷎ of alle halewen[3], of þat ilk᷎ kniȝth ;
His name is nempned here-bifore ;
I dreamt on a Tuesday before Nov. 1, of Edw. II,
Blissed be þe tyme þat he was bore !
who shall be chosen Emperor of Christendom.
ffor we shullen þe day see,
Emperour ychosen he worþe of cristiente. 48
God vs graunte þat ilk᷎ bone,
þat þilk᷎ tydyng here we sone
Of sir Edward oure derworþ kyng᷎

---

[1] A.S. *wiðer*, against ; *wiðerweard*, contrary, adverse.
[2] Decollation of John the Baptist, Aug. 29.—Nicolas.
[3] All Hallows, or All Saints' Day, Nov. 1.—Nicolas.

Ich mette of hym anoþere fair metyng· : 52
To oure lorde of heuene ich telle þis,
þat my sweuene tourne to mychel blis.
Me þou3th he rood vpon an Asse—   *I dreamt that Edw. II rode as a*
And þat ich take god to witnesse !—   56 *pilgrim towards Rome on an ass,*
ywonden he was in a Mantel gray ;
Toward Rome he nom his way ;
Vpon his heuede sat· an gray hure ;   *a gray cap on his head,*
It semed hym wel a mesure ;   60
he rood wiþouten hose & sho,—   *no hose or shoes on,*
his wone was nou3th so forto do ;—
his shankes semeden al blood rede ;   *but his shanks blood red.*
Myne herte wop for grete drede ;   64
Als a pilgryme he rood to Rome,
And þider he com wel swiþe sone.

Þ E þrid sweuene me mette a ni3th,   *The Third Dream.*
   Ri3th of þat derworþe kni3th ;   68
   þe wedenysday a ni3th it was,   *On Wednesday before Dec. 13*
Next· þe day of seint lucie¹ bifore cristenmesse.
Ich shewe þis, god of heuene :
To mychel ioye he tourne my sweuene !   72
Me þou3th þat ich was at· Rome,   *I dreamt I was at Rome,*
And þider ich com swiþe sone :
þe Pope², & sir Edward oure kyng·,   *and saw the Pope and Edw. II*
Boþe hij hadden a newe dubbyng· ;   76
Hure gray was her cloþing· ;   *with only gray caps on.*
Of oþere cloþes sei3 ich noþing·.
þe pope² 3ede bifore, mytred wel faire I-wys ;   *The Pope went first, in his mitre;*
þe kyng· Edward com corouned myd gret blis ;   80 *Edw. II was crowned, in token that he shall be the Emperor of Christendom.*
þat bitokneþ he shal be
Emperour in cristianete :
Iesus crist ful of grace,
Graunte oure kyng·, in euery place,   84
Maistrie of his wiþerwynes³,

¹ 'Lucy. Virgin and Martyr, Dec. 13.'—Nicolas.
² 'pope' *crosst through.* ³ A.S. *wiðerwynna*, adversary, enemy.

The fourth Dream.	And of alle wicked sarasynes!	
	Me met¹ a sweuene, on worþing-niȝth¹.	
	Of þat ilche derworþe kniȝth;	88
	God ich it shewe, & to witnesse take,	
I was in a chapel of the Virgin Mary.	And so shilde me fro synne & sake!	
	In-to an chapel ich com of oure lefdy;	
	I*esus* crist, hire leue son, stood by;	92
	On rode he was, an louelich Man,	
	Als þilk þat on rode was don.	
Christ vnnaild his hands from the Cross,	He vnneiled his honden two,	
	And seide, 'wiþ þe kniȝth he wolde go':	96
and askt his Mother's leave	"Maiden, & moder, & mylde quene,	
	Ich mote my kniȝth to-day sene.	
	Leue moder, ȝiue me leue,	
	ffor ich ne may no lenger bileue;	100
to go with Edw. II, who was going on a Crusade.	Ich mote conueye þat ilk¹ kniȝth,	
	þat vs haþ serued day and niȝth:	
	In pilerinage he wil gon,	
	To bien awreke of oure fon."	104
Christ's Mother gave him leave, as Edw. II had always servd her.	"Leue son, ȝoure wille, so mote it be,	
	for þe kniȝth boþe day & niȝth haþ s*er*ued me,	
	Boþe at¹ oure wille wel faire I-wys,	
	þerfore he haþ s*er*ued heuene-riche blis."	108
	God þat is in heuene so briȝth,	
	Be wiþ oure kyng¹ boþe day & niȝth!	
	Amen, Amen, so mote it¹ be!	
	þ*er*to biddeþ a pater n*oste*r & an Aue.	112
Adam, the Marshal of Stratford-at-Bow, dreamt this Dream,	¶ Adam, þe marchal, of stretford-atte-bowe—	
	Wel swiþe wide his name is yknowe,—	
	He hym-self¹ mette þis metyng¹—	
	To witnesse he takeþ I*es*u heuene kyng¹,—	116
on Wednesday in Lent.	On Wedenysday in clene leinte	
	A voice me bede I ne shulde nouȝth feinte;	
	Of þe sweuenes þat her ben write,	
	I shulde swiþe don my lorde kyng¹ to wite.	120

¹ I can't find what or when this is.

Ich ansuerde, 'þat I ne miȝtł for derkˈ gon.'
þe vois me bad goo, for liȝth ne shuld ich faile non,   *A voice from heaven bade me tell the King my dream.*
And þat I ne shulde lette for noþing',
þat ich shulde shewe þe kyng my metyng'.   124
fforþ ich wentˈ swiþe onon,
Estward as me þouȝth ich miȝth gon :
þe liȝth of heuene me com to,
As ich in my waye shulde go.   128
"Lorde, my body ich ȝelde þee to,
What ȝoure wille is wiþ me to do.
Ich take to witnesse god of heuene,
þat soþlich ich mette þis ilche sweuene[1] !   132
I ne reiche what ȝee myd my body do,
Als wisselich Iesus of heuene my soule vndergo."

þE þursday next þe beryng' of oure lefdy[2],   *The fifth Dream.*
Me þouȝth an Aungel com sir Edward by :   136
þe Aungel bitookˈ sir Edward on honde ;
Al bledyng' þe foure forþer clawes so were of þe lombe.
At Caunterbiry, bifore þe heiȝe autere, þe kyng' stood,   *I dreamt that Edw. II stood before the High Altar at Canterbury, clad all in red.*
ycloþed al in rede : murre he was of þat blee red as blood.
God, þat was on gode-friday don on þe rode,   141
So turne my sweuene niȝth & day to mychel gode !
Tweye poyntȝ þere ben þat ben vnshewed,   [leaf 27, back]
ffor me ne worþe to clerk ne lewed ;   144
Bot to sir Edward oure kyng',
hym wil ich shewe þilkˈ metyng'.
¶ Ich telle ȝou forsoþe wiþouten les,
Als god of heuene maide marie to moder ches,   148
þe Aungel com to me, Adam Dauy, & sede,   *An Angel bade me, Adam Davy, tell my dream to King Edward.*
"Botˈ þou, Adam, shewe þis, þee worþe wel yuel mede !"
þerfore, my lorde sir Edward þe kyng',
I shewe ȝou þis ilkˈ metyng',   152
As þe Aungel it shewed me in a visioun.

[1] "The Lady protests too much, methinks."—*Hamlet*, III. ii. 240.
[2] Nativity of the Virgin Mary, Sept. 8.—Nicolas.

1. ADAM DAVY'S 5 DREAMS ABOUT EDWARD II.

Unless my dreams come true, put me in prison!

Bot' þis tokenyng' bifalle, so dooþ me in-to prisoun!
Lorde, my body is to ȝoure wille [1];
þeiȝ ȝee willeþ me þerfore spille,   156
Ich it wil take in þolemodenesse,
Als god graunte vs heuene blisse;
And lete vs neuere þerof mysse,
þat we ne moten þider wende in clennesse!   160
Amen, amen, so mote it be,
And lete vs neuere to oþere waye tee!

I, Adam the Marshal, am known in Stratford-at-Bow and everywhere else.

Who so wil speke myd me, Adam þe marchal,
In stretforþe-bowe he is yknowe, & ouere al.   164
Ich ne shewe nouȝth þis forto haue mede,
Bot' for god almiȝtties drede;
    ¶ ffor it is sooþ.

[Follows, *The Jest of Alisaunder*, printed in Weber's *Romances*, vol. i.

"Diuers is þis myddellerede
    To lewed' Men & to lerede;
    Bysynesse / care & sorouȝ
    Is myd Man vche morowȝe." (&c.)]

[1] MS. willelle.

The Legend or Life of St. Alexius,

IN FOUR VERSIONS,

FROM SIX MANUSCRIPTS.

---

1. The longest version, in 12-line stanzas, from Laud MS. 622, in the Bodleian.
2. The shortest version, in couplets, from the Cotton MS., Titus A xxvi, in the British Museum.
3. The shorter 6-line-stanza version, from the grand Vernon MS. (ab. 1400 A.D.) and Laud 108, both in the Bodleian.
4. The longer 6-line-stanza version, from Laud MS. 463 in the Bodleian, and Trin. Coll. MS. Oxford 57 [81].

[THE first following version of the *Life of St Alexius*, from Laud 622, is the longest—and latest, no doubt[1],—of the English forms of the story. It was unknown to Dr Horstmann when he edited his *Altenglische Legenden*; and he having calld my attention to the other three versions of the Alexius legend, I have, for completeness' sake, added them here. I have also printed the Laud 108 opposite the Vernon text, from which it differs slightly sometimes in words, and in more distinctly Midland forms (*waster*, was there, l. 10; *hauest tou*, l. 490; *and tou*, l. 496; *and te*, l. 547; some *a* forms, like *gan*, l. 168), for convenience of comparison of two later representatives of one unknown original. I should perhaps apologize for wasting so much space on a mere legend of a so-calld saint's life. But the present story is the same pathetic one as Guy of Warwick's; it is prettily versified; and the comparing of the four ways in which the same incidents are told, has a certain interest: one likes to see how the religious-story writers of old spun out or shortend their material[2]: and the oddness of their notions as to the line of his images' life that pleasd the God and Father of men, is always instructive, specially when set beside many of the popular ideas on this and like subjects now. If folk would but stop attributing to God, motives, opinions, arrangements and likings, which they'd consider an insult to set down to any wise and good friend of their own, how much useless bother would come to an end!

Dr Horstmann,—who edited the Laud 108 Life in Herrig's *Archiv*, vol. iii. p. 102-10, 1873[3]—says that the sources of the Alexius legend are the '*Vita metrica*, auctore Marbodo, primum archidiacono Andegavensi, deinde Redonensi episcopo († 1123)', printed in the Acta Sanctorum, Boll. 17. Juli, p. 254-256; and another '*Vita*, auctore anonymo', ib. p. 251-254. To the last, the Laud 108 version is nearly related, often even in words. Eight Middle High German versions of this Legend were edited by Massmann, Quedlinburg, 1843. The following Early English lives do not belong to the great Collection of long-line "Saints' Lives" in the Harleian, Vernon, and other MSS, from which I printed a selection[4] for the Philological Society in 1863 for its *Transactions*, of 1858. This Collection will be edited in a separate volume some day for the E. E. Text Society, by Dr Horstmann, after he has edited for us all the Extra Legends not in the Collection or in the Vernon Gospel-stories.]

[1] There is a MS. of the Life in the Durham Cathedral Library, but my enquiries about it have not yet elicited any answer.
[2] Note how the shorter versions lengthen the end of the story.
[3] I believe that he has since edited the Vernon, Trinity and Laud-463 texts.
[4] And mistakingly printed 'i⸓' as Midland or Northern 'ic', instead of the Southern 'ich'.

THE LEGEND OR LIFE OF ST. ALEXIUS.

FROM SIX MANUSCRIPTS.

[*Laud MS.* 622, *leaf* 21, *back.*]

(1)

Alle þat willen here in ryme
Hou gode Men in olde tyme
Loueden god almiȝth, 3
þat weren riche of grete valoure,
Kynges sones and Emperoure,
Of bodies stronge & liȝth : 6
ȝee habbeþ yherd ofte in geste
Of holy men maken feste
Boþe daye & niȝth, 9
fforto haue þe ioye in heuene
wiþ Aungels song & mery steuene,
þere blis is brode & briȝth. 12

(2)

¶ To ȝou alle, heiȝe & lowe,
þe riȝth soþe to biknowe
ȝoure soules forto saue, 15
þe self waye þat god ȝede
To folowe hym I wolde ȝou rede,
heuene forto craue ; 18
And so duden þapostles alle,
þat to Iesu wolden calle,
ffor nouȝth þai nolde bilaue, 21
And to penaunce þai hem took,
werldes wele þai al forsook
Oure lordes loue to haue 24

(3)

¶ þise oþere holy seintz & gode,
Martirs, virgines mylde of mode,
And þise confessoures, 27
Religious þat her lijf willen diȝth,
fforto seruen god almiȝth
By tides & by houres ; 30
ȝee haue yherd saide wel ofte
Man may nouȝth lede lijf to softe,
And wonen in heuene boures. 33
þe godspel seiþ we moten lete
werldes lijf, þat þinkeþ vs swete,
And suffren hard shoures, 36

(4)

¶ ffader & moder & werldes goode,
And folowe hym þat dyed on rode
ffor oure synnes sake ; 39
And þan shullen we haue his loue,
And ioye & blis wiþ hym a-boue
þat he for vs gan make. 42
I shal ȝou now telle wiþ mouþe
Of on þat is name couþe
þat suffred woo & wrake. 45
his holy lijf & his godenesse
I may tellen more & lesse,
In woo hou he gan wake. 48

(5)
¶ he forsook᷎ confort᷎ of al his kynde,
Richesse he lete al bihynde,
To god al he hym took᷎: 51
Alexius is his name in storie,
writen of whom is made memorie
In many holy book᷎. 54
In Rome, þat was noble Cite,
woned a Man of grete pouste,
þat mychel mirþe a¹ wook᷎; 57
LAUD 622   [¹ MS. of a]

his lijf he lad worschiplich,
honoured he was of pouere & riche
þat on hym gan look᷎. 60
(6)
¶ Eufeniens was his name;
Of godenesse was his fame
In þe Cite of Rome. 63
þerfore þe riche Emperoure
Of þe Cite made hym Cenatoure.
ffor loos of his wisdome. 66
LAUD 622

[*MS. Cotton, Titus, A xxvi, lf.* 145.]
THE LYFE OF ST. ALEXES.
[A]lle þat wolle a whyle here dwell,
herkynnythe, and I woll yowe tell.
A tale Sone of grete pyte:
Att rome, by-ffell in þat Cyte, 4
COTTON   COTTON

[*Vernon MS., leaf* 44.]

Sitteþ stille with-outen strif,
   And i wol tellen ou of a lyf
   Of an holy Mon; 3
   Alix was his nome. [schome,
   To seruen god þhuȝte him no
þer-of neuer he ne blon. 6
his fadur was a gret lording,
Of rome a kyngus euenyng,
VERNON

[*Laud MS.* 108, *leaf* 233, *back.*]
VITA CUIUSDAM SANCTI VIRI
NOMINE ALEX. OPTIMA VITA.

Sitteþ stille wiþouten strif,
   And I schal telle ȝou þe lif
   Of an holy man. 3
   Alex was his ryȝtte name;
   To serue god þoute him no schame,
& þerof neuere he ne blan. 6
his fader was a gret lording
Of rome, a kynges euening,
LAUD 108

[*Laud MS.* 463, *leaf* 116.]

Lesteneþ alle & herkeneþ me,
   ȝong᷎ & olde, thewe & freo,
   And I. ȝou telle sone, 3
hou a ȝong᷎ man, gent & freo,
Bigan þe werldes wele to fleo,
y-bore was in Rome. 6
In Rome was a doughty man,
þat was cleped᷎ Eufemyan,
LAUD 463

[*Trin. Coll. MS., Oxf.,* 57 [81], *lf* 73.]
Vita Sancti Allexij.

Lesteneþ alle, and herkeneþ me,
   ȝonge and olde, bonde & fre,
   And ich ȝow telle sone, 3
How a ȝong᷎ man, gent and fre,
By-gan þis worldis wele to fle:
Y-born he was in Rome. 6
¶ In Rome was a doȝty man, [lf 73, bk]
þat was y-clepud Eufemian.
TRINITY

Riche he was of grete honoures,
Of londes, Castels, & of toures;
Men speken of hym ylome   69
In alle þinges wiþouten strijf¹;
Vche man he tauȝtte holy lijf¹
To his court þat come.   72

(7)

¶ Stronge he was in armes & liȝth,
Aȝeins Erle, baroun, & kniȝth,
his lordes riȝth to defende;   75

LAUD 622

þerfore hym loued þe Emperoure,
And made hym maister & gouern-
  oure
Of his tresore to spende.
To his somouns in armes clers
Two þousandes he had of bachelers,
þat curteis weren & hende,   81
And alle yshredd in cloþes of golde,
None fairer miȝtten ben on molde,
In þe werldes ende.   84

LAUD 622

There somtyme wonnyd a man,
hys name was callyd eufemyan;
he was ryche in all thyng,
And euery day seruyd as a kyng;   8
he had I-nowȝe of worlldys well,

COTTON

And seruantes with hym many and
  fele,
Thre thowesant to hym were atend-
  aund,
That weryd gold on here pendaunt.

COTTON

---

and hihte Eufemian.   9
Pore men to cloþe and fede,
In al rome, þat riche þeode,
such nas þer nan.   12

eueri day were in his halle
I-leid þreo bordus, forte calle
pore Men to fede.   15
Hem to serue he was wel glad;
he dude as iesu crist him bad;
he hoped þerfore to haue mede.   18

VERNON

& hyȝtte sire Eufemian.   9
Pore men to cloþe & fede,
In al rome, þat riche þede,
Swich ne waster non.   12

Eche day were in his halle
Leyd þre bordes, forto calle
Pore men to fede.   15
Hem to serue he was wel glad,
& dede as Iesu crist him bad;
þerfore he hopede han mede.   18

LAUD 108

Man of mychel myghte;   9
Gold & Siluer he hadde .y.-nouh,
Halles & boures, oxen & plouh,
And wonder wel it dyghte.   12
¶ ffor all þe seke of þe burhg¹
ffaste were y.-sough[t] þoruhg¹,
& brouht to his house.   15
he let hem bedde wel & fede,
And to hem tok¹ goed hede,
him-self & his spouse.   18

LAUD 463

Man of moche myȝte,   9
Gold and seluer he hadde y-nouȝ;
Halle and boures, oxse and plouȝ,
And swiþe wel it dyȝte,   12
ffor alle þe sike of þe borgh,
ffaste þeȝ were y-souȝt þorgh,
And i-broȝt to his house;   15
¶ And set hem bedde wel & fede,
And to hem toke guod hede,
Him-selue & eke his spouse.   18

TRINITY

(8)
¶ Men þat ȝeden in pilerinage
And Men of ordre¹, was his vsage
Often forto fede. [¹ MS. oydre] [leaf 22] 87
Dame Agloes hiȝth his spouse,
Her dedes weren wel preciouse
Holy lijf to lede.   90
She was fair honeste & wijs,
Louelich, & of gret' prijs,
Ycome of gode kynrede;   93
       LAUD 622

Aȝeins no Man she mystook',
wiþ contenaunce ne wiþ look',
Noiþer in word' ne dede.   96
(9)
¶ Barayne was þat gode wijf',
In sorouȝ she ledde her lijf',
ffor she no childe hadde.   99
hir lorde for þat ilk' þinge
Ofte his honden gan to wrynge,
And sorouȝful lijf' he ladde;   102
       LAUD 622

In hys owne hous euery daye,   13
A custyume was that I schall saye:
there boredes that were fayre spred,
There pormen schulde be fede;   16
Of all pormen of ylk a gate,
there was none þat werned þe yate.
       COTTON

A wyfe he had, she hyght a gales,
An holey woman withowten lees; 20
She louyd god with all her myght,
And seruyd hym bothe daye and nyght;
She was of gode wyll, and hart Free
To all þe dedes of charite.   24
       COTTON

---

whon he was serued bi and bi,
þenne was he redi
to go to his mete;   21
ffor þe loue of Godes sone,
wiþ Men of Religione
wolde he sitte and ete.   24
¶ His wyf hiȝte dame Agloes,
to sigge soþ with-oute les,
þat muche was to preyse.   27
       VERNON

When þei were serued by & by,
þane at arst was he redy
To gon to his mete;   21
þanne in drede of godes sone,
Wiþ men of religione
He wolde sitte & ete.   24
His wif hyȝtte dame Agles,
To seye þe soþe wiþoute les,
þat meche was to preyse;   27
       LAUD 108

þe man hadde a god' wif,
She ne louede flyt' ne stryf
In al hire liue.   21
þe sekemen ofte she fedde,
& softe brouȝt' hem obedde,
blessed' beo she to wiue.   24
¶ þei were to-gedere ȝeres two,
& so þei were somdel mo,
With-outen any blede.   27
       LAUD 463

þis man hadde a wel guod wyf;
Hy ne louede fyȝt ne stryf
In al here lyue.   21
þe sike men wel ofte hy fedde,
And broȝte hem to hare bedde:
I-blessed be hy to wyue!   24
¶ Hy were to-gyderes ȝeres two,
And so þeȝ were somdel mo,
With-oute eny blede.   27
       TRINITY

ffor he wende þat god almiʒth
had ben wrooþ wiþ hym apliʒth,
þereof sore hym dradde. 105
Ofte he bisouʒth god in heuene
Sende hem a childe, wiþ mylde steuene,
To maken hem bliþe & gladde, 108

(10)
¶ Conforte of hym forto haue,
her godes after hem to saue,

LAUD 622

her londes & her ledes; 111
her eyre of hym forto make,
And her richesse hym bitake,
Palfreies & her stedes. 114
Ofte þai maden þus her bone,
And god sent' hem grace sone,
þat fulfilde were þoo dedes: 117
A son conceyued þat gode wijf';
Tyme com in her olde lijf'
ybore it most be nedes. 120

LAUD 622

---

there she wolde clothe and fede,
and helpe men at here nede.
By twene theym chyllde had þey none,
there fore they made mykell mon. 28
theye were allwaye blythe and hende,
In hope that god sholde hem sende

COTTON

[1] Some maydyn chyllde, or some man, [1 lf 145, bk]
That theyre herytages myght hane;
So long theye prayed with good entent, 33
that a man chyllde god hem sent;

COTTON

But heo dede þe same manere
as dede hir lord, as ʒe may here,
was heo nout at ese. 30
Children bi-twene hem hedde þei none,
þer-of to god þei maden heor mone
boþe dai & niht. 33
Iesu crist herde her bone,
& sende hem a ful good sone,
heor herte forte liht. 36

VERNON

Bote ʒe myʒtte do þe same maner
þat dede hire lord, as y seyde er,
Was ʒe nat wel atayse. 30
[1] Child hem bi-twene ne hadde þei non;
þer-fore to god he maden here mon,
Boþe be day & nyʒthe; [1 leaf 234] 33
Iesu crist herde here bone,
& sente hem a ful god sone,
here hertes forto lyʒthe. 36

LAUD 108

þei bede god with herte gode,
þat hem sende suich a fode
to serue hem & drede. 30
And Iesu Crist, þat is so mylde,
ʒaf hem grace, she was with chylde,
þe gode lauedye. 33
Boþe be day, & be nyght,
ʒerne þei þonked our' dright,
& Seinte Marie. 36

LAUD 463

þeʒ bede god with herte guode,
þat hem sende such a fode,
To seruy him & drede. 30
And iesu crist, þat is so mylde,
Hem ʒaf grace hy was with childe,
þat guode Leuedye. 33
¶ Bothe be daye & eke be nyʒte,
Wel ʒerne hy þonkede oure dryʒte,
And so hy dede Marie. 36

TRINITY

(11)

¶ þai þankeden god, & glade were,   þe childe was mery iᴺ al manere,
And avoweden in þis manere   As þai maden her praiere,
Chastite boþe to take,   123   Aniȝth as þai gan wake.   129
And to lyuen in clene lijfᵗ,   Alexius þai gonnen hym calle;
Eufeniens & his gode wijfᵗ,   yloued he was amonges hem alle
And synne to forsake.   126   þat to hym gonnen take.   132
          LAUD 622   LAUD 622

---

whan they wyst þat hit was so,   Fayne were here frendys therforne;
Chanse theye leuyd bothe twoo, 36   Theye bare the chylde to chirche A
Sythyn þey wolde for no need   none,   41
Com to gedur in Flesschely ded.   And crystenyd hyt in the Font
Whan thys man chyllde was borne,   stone.
          COTTON   COTTON

---

¹So sone was bore þat blisful child,   When he was bore, þat blisful child,
Alix boþe meke and Mild, [¹ leaf 44, bk]   Alex, boþe mek & myld,
and of maners hende.   39   And of maneres hende: 39
sone after wiþ gret hast,   A litel after, wiþ greth hast
þei Auouwede boþe chast   þei a-voweden to him chast,
to heore lyues ende.   42   To here lyues ende.   42
          VERNON   LAUD 108

¶ þo þe child y.-bore was,   þo þis child y-bore was,
þei þonked Crist of his grace   Crist þeȝ þonkede of þat cas,
wiþ glad chiere.   39   With wel glade chere.   39
Also as þe wone was,   Al-so as þe wone was,
As þei coude with softe pas,   As hy couþe with softe pas
to chirche þei it bere.   42   þat child to cherche bere.   42
// þo þis child to chirche com,   ¶ þo þis child to cherche com,
To afong Cristendom,   To vnderfonge cristendom,
as þe ryght is,   45   As riȝt it is,   45
his fader & his moder þo   His fader & his moder bo,
Swiþe bliþe were bo,   Swiþe blithe were þo,
& cleped it Alexijs.   48   And clepude it 'allexis.'   48
¶ þei nadde bot þilk sone,   ¶ Hy nadde bote þat ilke sone,
therfore as it is þe wone,   þerfore, as it is þe wone,
þei loued it þe more.   51   Hy louede him þe more.   51
þo he was old, ȝeres seueñ,   ¶ þo he was old ȝeres seuene,
þei him wissed with mylde steueñ,   þeȝ wissede him with mylde steuene,
& sette him to lore.   54   And sette him to lore¹. [¹ MS. sore] 54
          LAUD 463   TRINITY

(12)

¶ Alexius was sett' to boke,
To gode maistres þai hym toke,
And wise of clergie. 135
þe more he wex in elde & lengþe,
To seruen god he dude his strengþe
And his moder Marie. 138

LAUD 622

To þe Emperour whan he was brouȝth
þere dedes of Armes weren ywrouȝth
To lernen chiualrye; 141
þere miȝth he sen in tour[na]ment
what kniȝth was douȝttiest of dent'
And man of most maistrie. 144

LAUD 622

---

there theye callyd þe chylde Alexe;
Sone hit throofe, and wele hit wex.
Whan hit was vij yere olde and more,
hys freendys sett hym wnto lore; 46
he was sone Full goode of wytt,

COTTON

And wnderstode the holy wryte;
he loued god in all his thought, 49
And of thys worllde gaffe he nought;
he sawe thys worllde was butt gylle,
for hit showld laste but a whyle; 52

COTTON

þer-aftur was hit not longe,
Alix couþe speke and gonge,
and was i-set to lere; 45
sone he was a wel god clerk,
& muche he loued godus werk
forte speke & here. 48

VERNON

þer-after was it nat lange:
Alex coude speke & gange,
And was set to lere. 45
Sone he was a ful good clerk,
& meche he louede godes werk
fforto speke & here. 48

LAUD 108

¶ Þis child wex & wel they,
Cristes help him was ney,
& þat was wel y.-sene; 57
for more he lerned in on ȝer
þan any of his oþer fere
dide in ȝeres tene. 60
// As sone as he vnderstod
Werldes blisse nas not god,
Who it vnderstode, 63
Werldes wele he forsok',
& to Iesu Crist him tok',
þat deyede on þe Rode. 66
// he besought nyght & day
heueñ king', þat al wel may,
ȝeue him strength & mygh[t]e 69
Aȝein þe feond þat is aboute,
to bring' his soule in gret doute,
· gostliche to fighte. 72

LAUD 463

Þis child wax, and wel y-þeȝ,
Cristis help him was neȝ,
And þat was wel y-sene; 57
ffor more he lernede² in one ȝere
þan eny of his oþere fere
Dede in ȝeres tene. [² MS. sernede] 60
¶ ffor sone þis child him vnderstod
þis worldis blisse was noȝt guod,
þe man þat him vnderstode, 63
Worldes wele he forsoke,
And to iesu crist him toke,
þat do was on þe rode. 66
He by-soȝte nyȝt and day
Heuene kynge, þat al þynge may,
He ȝeue him strengþe & myȝte 69
¶ Aȝens þe fend þat is a-boute,
To brynge vs in euel route,
Gostlich to fyȝte. 72

TRINITY

(13)
¶ His fader was boþe wijs & ware,
ffor þat his son so wel hym bare,
he loued hym al his lijfᵗ. 147
he þouȝth to don swiche puruyaunce,
whar-wiþ he miȝth hym avaunce
And wynne hym a wijfᵗ. 150
To a riche prince his son he sentᵗ,
And afterward to hym he wentᵗ,
Stille wiþouten strijfᵗ : 153
LAUD 622

A douȝtter he had, briȝth & shene,
þe heritage shulde hires bene
Of Castel & londes rijfᵗ. 156
(14)
¶ whan ayþer herd oþeres wille,
And speken þerof to-gedre stille
To make þat sposaile, 159
Of þe tyme comen was þe day
To fulfille wiþouten delay,
Certeyn, wiþouten faile, 162
LAUD 622

---

neuerthe les whan he was elde,
lone and felde For to wellde,
hys fader puruyde hym a wyffe, 55
Wit whome he soulde led hys lyffe ;
A mayden there was fayre and Fre,
Com of þe rycheste of that cette. [lf 146]
COTTON

In holy chyrche vppon a daye 59
They were spousyde in goddys laue ;
Atte here spousyng I wott there stode
Beshoppys felle and prestes goode ;
Sythen theye made a mangery
With all the beste of here aleye ; 64
COTTON

As time as he bi-gon to belde,
and was i-come to Monnes elde,
him was chosen a wyf, 51
VERNON

Sone whan he gan to belde,
& forto comen to mannes elde,
him was chosen a wif, 51
LAUD 108

¶ his bone herde þe Kingᵗ of heuen,
& spakᵗ to him wiþ mylde steuene,
& seide, 'Alexijs, 75
To-day þou may bliþe beo,
þi bone I. grante þe,
& a sete in heuen blisse. 78
¶ Andᵗ .I. þe do to vnderstonde,
þat þou most þole shame & shonde,
al for my sake. 81
Into vnkouþ lond þou mostᵗ wende,
Sone I. wile þe þider sende,
& al þi kin forsake. 84
Into vnkouþ londᵗ þou shalt fare,
& suffre myche tene & care,
& al for loue myn ; 87
& sithen þou shaltᵗ aȝein come,
& in þi fader hous wone,
& þer-in haue goedᵗ fyn.' 90
LAUD 463

His bone y-herde þe kynge of heuene,
And spake to him with mylde steuene,
And seyde, 'allexis, 75
To-day þou myȝt wel blyþe be,
ffor þyne bone ich granty þe,
And my blessynge y-wis. 78
¶ And ich þe do wel to vnderstonde
þat þou most þolye shame & shonde,
Al for myne sake. 81
Into vncouþe londe þou most wende,
Sone þuder ich wil þe sende,
And al þy ken forsake. 84
In-to vncouþ lond þou most fare, [lf 74]
And soffry moche tene þare,
Al for sone myne. 87
¶ And suþþe þou shelt a-ȝe come,
And in þy fader hous [shalt] wone,
And þer-ynne fyne.' 90
TRINITY

ST. ALEXIUS IS MARRIED AGAINST HIS WILL.

To þe chirche of seint Bonefas
wiþ þis maiden þai token þe pas,
þat heiȝe was of paraile ; 165
As custume was & shulde be,
þai maden gret solempnite,
þe Pope & his conseile. 168

(15)
¶ Alexius was shamefast',
And of weddyng' he was agast',
his vijs al pale bywent' ; 171

LAUD 622

Leuer hym were to be ded
þan haue ytrowed þat ilk' red
By his owen assent'. 174
He ne wist what he miȝth don ;
fful gret sorouȝ com hym on,
he helde hym-self' shent'. 177
To god he gan hym al affye,
And to his moder seint Marie,
Trewely, wiþ gode entent'. 180

LAUD 622

All that comyn thyder þat daye
theye were seruyd welle to paye,
Com þey erley, com the late,
theye wer neuer wernyd þe yate ; 68
there was nowder man nor knaue,
Byt mete and drynke he myght haue.

COTTON

Euery man had there plente
Of claret wyne and pymente ; 72
There was many a riche wyne,
In syllurer and in golde fyne ;
Many a coppe and many a pece,
with wyne wernage & eke of grece ;

COTTON

Out of þe Emperors bour,
a maiden god with gret honour,
to wedden wiþ-oute strif. 54

VERNON

Out of þe emperoures bour,
A mayde good, of greth honur,
To wedde wiþ-oute strif. 54

LAUD 108

¶ þe childes fader fel in elde,
& his moder godes helde
ȝeres hadde fele. 93
he wold his sone shold wiue,
To glade hem in her' liue,
& haue werldes wele. 96
þei sought' hem sone a mayde,
þat witty was, as al folk' sayde,
comen of hy kinne. 99
Womman she was of heu bright,
heo þouht' on crist day & nyht,
& kepte hir' fro sinne. 102
þo þei wer' to-gidere come,
þis maide & þis ȝong' gom,
In godes lawe, 105
þere was game & myche gleo,
Ac, for-soþe, tel I. þe,
eyled him no plawe. 108

LAUD 463

þis childis fader fel on elde,
And his moder godis helde,
ȝeres hadde fele. 93
Hy wolde here sone sholde wyue,
To gladen hem in þis lyue,
And haue worldis wele. 96
¶ Hy by-soȝten him a mayde,
þat witty was and ful of rede,
I-come of heȝe kenne ; 99
Woman hy was of hewe briȝt,
Hy þoȝte on crist day and nyȝt,
And wiste here fro senne. 102
ffor þo hy were to-gydere y-come,
þis mayde and þis ȝonge gome,
In godis lawe, 105
¶ þer was game and moche gle,
Ac, al for-soþe ich telle þe,
Ne eysede hem no plawe. 108

TRINITY

ST. ALEXIUS IS BID GO TO HIS WIFE IN BED.

(16)
¶ Napeles he lete his heuynysse,
And made mychel ioye & blisse
At þat solempnite.   183
He bare hym curteislich & stille,
To fulfille his faders wille,
Glad as he had ybe.   186
ffulfild was þe weddyng¹
wiþ ioye & blis in al þing¹,
þat many man miȝth see.   189
LAUD 622

þe niȝth was comen, & þe day gon,
þe kniȝttes waten on & on
To her owen cuntre.   192
(17)
¶ Eufeniens his son gan calle,
And tidynges amonge hem alle
He tolde hym þat were newe.   195
'Son, to þi chaumbre þou most wende,
To þi wijf fair & hende,   [leaf 22, back]
Blysful & briȝth of hewe.'   198
LAUD 622

And many A noder ryche vessell
with wyne of gascoyne and of rochell.
whan euyne com þat elke a gest
was gone to bed to take hys rest,   80
COTTON

Eufemyan callyd hys sone Anone,
And bad hym þat he shoulde gone
In to hys chaumbur to hys fere,
And cowmfort her in hys manere.   84
COTTON

¶ whon heo weren weddet þe furste
in godus lawe as hit was riȝt, [niȝt,
& weren i-brouȝt to house,   57
Mekeliche he gon hire teche
to drede god of sunne is leche,
þat is Maidenes spouse.   60
VERNON

Whan þei were wedded þe ferste nyȝth
In godes [lawe], as it was ryȝth,
& was I-brouth to house :   57
Mek[e]liche he gan hire teche,
To drede god, of sinne leche,
þat is maydenes spouse.   60
LAUD 108

¶ þe day was go, þe nyht was com,
Seide þe fader to þe sone,
wiþ glad cher',   111
'vp arys, sone myn,
& go into boure þyn,
To glade þi fere.'   114
// þo he com to boure to his fere,
he beheld þe may of glad chere,
& of bright hewe.   117
Sone menged his þouht',
In fonding he was brouht,
his car' began al newe.   120
ne syȝte & made sory chere,
þe teres out of his wete lere
bitter he let falle.   123
Ne myht glade him his fere
with wordes ne with fair chere,
þat stod shred in palle.   126
LAUD 463

þe day was go, þe nyȝt was come ;
þo seyde þe fader to þe sone,
With wel glade chere,   111
'Op arys, þou sone myn,
And go [þou] in-to boure þyn,
To glady þyne fere.'   114
¶ þo he was in-to boure y-broȝt,
He by-held þat may swaþel & toȝt
Of briȝte hywe.   117
Sone turnde he his þoȝt,
In fondynge he was y-broȝt,
His care be-gan al nywe ;   120
He siȝte, & made sorweful chere,
Teres ouer his whyte lere
Bytere he let falle.   123
¶ Ne myȝte him gladye his fere,
With wordes ne with fayre chere,
þat stod y-shrud in palle ;   126
TRINITY

And whan Alixius herd þat word
It pricked his hert' as speres oord,
So sore it gan hym rewe ;   201
Bot his fader wrappi he nolde,
He had leuer be vnder molde,
þat neuer man hym knewe.   204

(18)
¶ whan þe folk' was went away,
And he al-one in chaumbre lay,
Alexius gan to preche ;   207
    LAUD 622

Of Iesu he bigan his game,
werldes likyng' he gan blame,
his ȝonge wijf to teche.   210
He tauȝtte hir, þat was so hende,
Hou she shulde haue god to frende
þat is oure soules leche ;   213
ȝif she wolde alle her lijf'
Duelle boþe maiden & wijf',
þe fende she miȝth do wreche.   216
    LAUD 622

Alex was to hym obedyent, [leaf 146, bk]
and ded his faders comawndement ;
In to a chaumbur he com full ryght,
And redy there he founde hys bryght,
    COTTON

And toke here in his armys twoo,
And downe they layde bothe twoo ;
'dame,' he sayde, 'nou it ys soo,
Of Flessche ar wee allso.   92
    COTTON

He preched hire with al his miht,
of sunne heo scholde haue no pliȝt,
but holden hir Maidenhed.   63
Of Iesu þat Maiden clene,
in whom was neuere wem i-sene,
heo schulde han hire med.   66
    VERNON

he prechede hire wiþ al his myȝth :
Of s[i]nne ȝe scholde hauen no plyȝth,
Bote kepe hire maydenhod ;   63
& of iesu, þat mayde clene,
In whom was neuere wem I-sene,
ȝe scholde habbe hire mede.   66
    LAUD 108

---

¹¶ No lenger to hele of he brak',
þe ȝongman to his bride spak',
with wel fair bere :   129
'Lemman, haue goday, [¹ leaf 116, back]
No lenger I ne may
wiþ þe leuen here.   132
// Wende I mot fer of lond,
& suffre tene & peines strong',
my sinnes to bete.   135
Boþe I. mot, for godesake,
ffader & moder myn forsak',
& þe þat art' so suete.'   138
// þo she hadde herde þis tale,
Al hir' blis turned to bale,
y-swowe she fel to gronde.   141
þo she of swounyng' ros,
Atterliche hir' agros
with care she was y-bound.   144
    LAUD 463

þo it alles op a brake,
þe ȝonge man to his brede spake,
With wel fayre bere :   129
'Leman, haue guod day,
No lenger ich ne may
With þe by sene here.   132
¶ Wende ich mot fer out of londe,
And soffry tene & peynes stronge,
My synnes to bete.   135
Bothe ich mot, for godis sake,
ffader & moder myne forsake,
And þe þat art so swete.'   138
þo hy hadde y-herd þe tale,
Hire blesse turnde to bale,
A-swoȝe hy fel to grounde.   141
¶ þo hy of swoȝenynge a-ros,
Wel sore here a-gros,
With care hy was y-bounde.   144
    TRINITY

ST. ALEXIUS RESOLVES TO LEAVE HIS WIFE A VIRGIN.

(19)
¶ þat maiden herkned swiþe stille,
And whan he seide hadd al his wille
þe holy gost hir lauȝtte, [moodᵈ
And she hym graunted wiþ mylde
To louen Iesu þat dyed [on] roodᵈ,
As he hym-self hir tauȝtte. 222
Alexius was þoo glad & bliþe,
his ioye couþe he noman kiþe,
his spouse a ryng⸱ he rauȝtte, 225

And seide to hir, 'my suete þing⸱,
Take to þee þis ilk⸱ ryng⸱,
And kepe it in þine auȝtte. 228
(20)
¶ 'Of me whan þou wilt haue mynde
Loke here-on, as þou art hende,
Boþe by day & niȝth. 231
In pilerynage now wil I go,
And half¹ þe godenesse þat I do
Graunte þee god almiȝth.' 234

LAUD 622   LAUD 622

Noue may we be gladde of þis lyffe,
For thowe art bothe moder and wyffe;
For attwaye rede þat hit so be, 95
For nowe muste me wende frome the.

Whylys I was yong I made a vowe,
That I wyll Fullfell hyt nowe,
For to wende a pylgremage,
Noue woll I doo þat vyage, 100

COTTON   COTTON

þenne tok he his gold ryng,
and ȝaf hit to þat Maide ȝing,
and seide to hire þus : 69
'Tac þis Ryng and kep hit me,
til þat godes wille be,
crist beo bi-twene vs.' 72

þanne tok he his gold ring,
& ȝaf þat mayde, þat was ȝing,
& seyde to hire þus : 69
'Tak þis ring, & kep it me,
Til þat godes wille be,
God bi-twene vs.' 72

VERNON   LAUD 108

¶ Sone þo she myht⸱ stonde,
She tar hir' heer, & wrong⸱ hir' hondᵈ,
& made reuful bere. 147
'Nou þou wilt⸱ my lef of londe,
Loke I. may after þe long⸱,
Alas, þat I. dedᵈ nere. 150
// Allas, mi lef, what hastou þouht,
Iu myche care þou hast me brouht⸱,
on me þou hast sinne. 153
After þat þou art gon,
Vpbreidᵈ me tyt manyon
of þi riche kinne. 156
// Awey, mi lef, þat I. was bore,
ffor al my blisse is forlore,
& nou waxeþ my pine. 159
Alone her-inne I. wile wone,
& euere eft⸱ mannes mone shone,
Al for loue þine.' 162

Sone so hy myȝte op-stonde,
Hy tar here her, & wrang⸱ here honde,
And made reuful bere : 147
'Now þou wilt lef out of londe,
Loky ich may after þe longe ;
Allas ! þat ich ded nere ! 150
¶ Allas my lef ! what hast þou þoȝt ?
In moche care ich am y-broȝt ;
Of me þou hast synne. 153
After þat þou art a-gon,
Op breyde me tyt of manyon,
Of þyne riche kynne ; 156
A-wey my lef, þat ich was y-bore,
ffor al my blisse is for-lore,
And now wexeþ my pyne. 159
¶ Allone her-ynne ich wille wonye,
¹And euere eft mannes mone shonye,
Al for loue þyne.' [¹ leaf 74, back] 162

LAUD 463   TRINITY

Alexius þus his leue tooke;
Rewely his wijf gan on hym loke
þat was so fair &¹ briȝth ;   [¹ MS. w]
She ne wist to what londe   238
þat she miȝth sende hym any sonde,
Doune fel þat swete wiȝth.   240

(21)

¶ Alixius from his richesse
In-to pouert' & wrecchednesse,
ffrom his frendes he fledde.   243

LAUD 622

vnto þe Cee he com wel sory,
A shippe he fonde to seil redy,
þe holy gost hym ledde.   246
Of his golde & of his pens
wel he aquited his despens,
hendely of þat he hedde.   249
þe wynde aroos at' her wille,
wheþer þai wolde, loude or stille;
At' her likyng' þai spedde.   252

LAUD 622

And þou schalt lewe here at home,
agayne as goddys wyll I come.'
he yaffe her a gyrdeH and a ryng,
aH for a tokyng at þeyre departyng;

COTTON

And Forthe he went that elke nyght.
To þe sse he come fuH ryght;
The shipe was redy, and ouer went,
wynde att wyH god hym sent.   108

COTTON

¶ whon he hedde don as i ou sei,
he tok his leue & went his wei
from þat Maiden fre.   75
A parti god with him he tok,
& al þat oþur he forsok,
and wende him to þe séé.   78

VERNON

Whanne he hadde ido, as [I] ȝou sey,
He tok his leue & wente his wey
fro þat mayde fre;   75
A parti of his good he wiþ him tok,
And al þat oþer he for-sok,
he wente to þe see.   78

LAUD 108

¶ 'Lemman, al for þi sake,—
So doþ þe turtel for hir' make
whan he is y.-slawe,—   165
Al myrthe I. wile forsake,
& euere-more sorwe take,
& shone al plawe.'   168
he tok' his girdel in his hond',
& his mantel þerwiþ he wond',
& his ring' of golde.   171
'Mi lemman, haue þis to þe,
& oþer while þenk' on me
Whan I. lye vnder molde.   174

¶ Gret wel fader & modur myn,
leue her'-inne, & beo her' hyne
with wel milde mode.   177
þilk' lord' .I. þe beteche,
þat is of alle bales leche,
& deþ þoled' on þe rode.'   180

LAUD 463

'Leman, al for þyne sake,—
So doþ þe drake for here make,
Whanne he is a-slawe,—   165
Alle merthe ich wille forsake,
And euere-more sorwe take,
And shonye alle plawe.'   168
¶ He nam his gerdul on his hond,
And his mantel þer-on he wond,
And his ryng' of golde.   171
'My leman, haue now þis to þe,
And oþer whyle þenk' on me,
whanne ich ligge vnder molde;   174

Gret wel fader & moder myn,
By-lef her-ynne, & serue him
With wel mylde mode.   177
¶ þulke lord ich þe by-teche,
þat is of alle bale leche,
þat deþ þolede on rode.'   180

TRINITY

(22)

¶ At a Cite Galys men calle
To londe þai gonnen aryuen alle,
wiþouten enpeirement. 255
Alexius of hem tooke leue,
And worschiplich þai hym ȝeue :
To chircheward he went. 258
He þanked god wiþ good wille
Erly & late, loude & stille,
þat þider hem hadde sent. 261

LAUD 622

He bisouȝth god, & gan to wepe,
þat from þe fende he shulde hym kepe
And his enticement. 264

(23)

¶ þus he þat had riche wedes,
Heiȝe hors, & gode stedes,
And Armes briȝth & shene, 267
Al he leet þe godes gret,
And went on his bare feet,
his soule to make clene. 270

LAUD 622

---

whan he come Into a Fer contre,

COTTON

he come into a ryche cytte, 110

COTTON

He fond schipes redi,
to on he wente priueli,
ouer forte fare. 81
whon he was ouere on þe sond,
he was in an vnkouþ lond,
þer he con neuer are. 84
He went him forþ with godus wille,
a feir cite he com tille,
þe nome i schal ou telle. 87
Edissa hette þe cite,
godus seruaunt forte be,
þerinne forte dwelle. 90

VERNON

He fond schipes redely ;
To on he wente priueli,
ouer forto fare ; 81
He seyde he was a chapman,
& preyde, he moste wiþ hem gon,
ȝif þat here schip were ȝare. 84
fforþ he wente wiþ godes wille ;
A fair cyte he com vn-tille ;
þe name I schal ȝou telle : 87
Edissa hatte þat cite ;
Godes seruant þer to be,
þer-inne wolde he dwelle. 90

LAUD 108

// Out of bour he went anon,
As swiþe as he myht gon,
Right to þe stronde. 183
Sone a ship he fond ȝare,
þat was redy to fare
Into vnkouþ lond. 186
¶ Into þe ship anon he wend,
& god suche wind sende
þat sone to lond hem brouht. 189
þat ship was god, þe watur deope,
& oþer while sore he wepe,
& was in gret þouht. 192

LAUD 463

Out of þe borgh he wente anon,
So swiþe so he myȝte gon,
Ryȝt to-ward þe stronde ; 183
Sone a schip he fond þare,
þat was redy to fare
In-to vncouþe londe. 186
¶ In-to þe schip anon he wente,
And god wel sone such a wynd sente,
þat to þe lond hem broȝte. 189
þat schip was guod, þat water dep,
And oþer whyle sore he wep,
And was in moche þoȝte ; 192

TRINITY

Ofte it fel in his mende		þere he duelled in grete pouerte,	
Of his fader & moder hende,		In hunger, in þorst, & oþer smerte,	
þat souȝth he schulde bene.	273	þat many man it sowe.	282
He wolde for none kynnes þing¹		þe Cee of grece passed he is,	
þat Men hadden of hym knouyng¹,		In-to þe Cite of Annys,	
þerfore he gan to flene.	276	He com þat ilk¹ þrowe.	285
(24)		God he bitauȝtte his compaignye,	
¶ ffrom þat cuntre swiþe he ȝede,		And ȝede to a chirche of seint Marie	
To-ward Surrie in feble wede,			
þat noman shulde hym knowe.	279	wiþ herte meke and lowe.	288
LAUD 622		LAUD 622	

¹Knowyn he woHde in no wyse be   Of no man þat shoullde hym see. 112
[¹ leaf 147]   COTTON   COTTON

þe goodus þat he wiþ him brouȝt		þe goodes þat he wiþ him brougth,	
of hem wolde he riȝt nouȝt,		Of hem ne wolde he ryȝth nowth,	
he ȝaf hem pore men.	93	Bote ȝaf hem pore menne;	93
His Robe he ȝaf þer he sauh nede,		his robe he ȝaf þer he sey nede,	
and cloþed him-self in pore wede,		& cloþede him-sulf in pore wede,	
for no mon scholde him ken.	96	ffor noman scholde him kenne.	96
He ede to A chirche hei,		he ȝede to a churche-ȝate,	
þer pore men seeten in þe wei,		þer pouere men sete in þe gate,	
Almus forte take.	99	Almesse forto take;	99
AMongus hem he sat a-doun,		Among hem he sat a-doun,	
and asked wiþ deuociun		& Askede wiþ deuocion	
sum god for Godus sake.	102	Sum good for godes sake.	102
VERNON		LAUD 108	

// þo he vp to londe com		þo he in-to þe lond com,	
he seld his cloþes euerichoñ,		He solde his cloþes euerichon,	
& bouȝt¹ him pore wede;	195	And boȝte him pouere wede.	195
And¹ his gold¹ & his feo		¶ Al his gold and al his fe,	
Among¹ þe pore delte he		Among¹ þe pouere delte he,	
þat hadde mych neode.	198	þat hadde moche nede;	198
¶ Sone he it vndernom̃,		Sone he it vnder-nom,	
þat he to a borugh com,		þat he to one borgh com,	
þat mychel was & kete.	201	þat moche was & kete.	201
Sone so he þider com̃		Sone so he þuder com,	
to þe temple þe weye he nom̃,		To þe temple he wente anon,	
God¹ selue to grete.	204	God self to grete.	204
LAUD 463		TRINITY	

ADAM DAVY.   3

(25)

¶ At þat chirche is an ymage
Of oure lefdy vpon a stage,
þat many man haþ souȝth. 291
It was ymaked of Aungels honde,
To def & doumbe of oþere londe
Miracle þere was wrouȝth. 294
Alexius was glad & bliþe,
His ioye couþe he noman kiþe,
In hert ne in þouȝth, 297
whan he miȝth seen in signe
Hou goddes ymage fair & digne
In his moders barme was brouȝth. 300

(26)

¶ Often he made his orisoune,
wepande wiþ deuocioune,
To þe quene of heuene, 303

LAUD 622

And seide, 'moder mylde & free,
Praie þi son of gret pouste
ffor his names seuene, 306
þat from heuene com to þee, [leaf 23]
By assent of þe trinite,
þorouȝ þe Aungels steuene, 309
Here to suffre many peynes
In al his body & his veynes,
In erþe as I can neuene, 312

(27)

¶ 'And þat he sheweþ in his
 mercy,
Marie, to þee I make my cry,
þat am a synful Man; 315
ffor wiþ his blood & peynes grene,
þe whiche to vs purchaced ene,
ffro helle he vs wan. 318

LAUD 622

In that cyte was an Image,
That was lyke goddes wysage, 114
Many a pylgryme had hit sought,
For hit was neuer with honde wrought.
Alex herd ther of than t[e]He,

COTTON

Than thought he there to dueH.
A none he yaffe Frome hym awaye
to powre men aH hys monaye; 120
And bought hym pore man ys
 wede,

COTTON

þat chirche was of vr ladi,
þer-Inne was a gret celli,
an ymage of hire sone, 105
Maked of a wonder werk,
þat nouþur lewed mon nor clerk
ne miȝt wite hou hit was done; 108
fforþi was þider gret sekyng
of on and oþur, old and ȝyng,
of al þat Cuntre, 111

VERNON

þat churche was of oure leuedy;
þer-inne was a greth selly,
An ymage of hire son, 105
Maked of a wonder werk, [leaf 234, bk]
þat neyþer lewed man ne clerk
Niste hou it was don. 108
þerfore was þider greth sekyng
Of on & oþer, old & ȝing,
Of al þat countre; 111

LAUD 108

Among þe pore he woned þar
In sorwe & in myche care,
til he fel to elde. 207

LAUD 463

¶ Among þe pouere he wonede þare,
In moche sorwe and moche care,
ffor-to he fel to elde. 207

TRINITY

Swete Iesu, heuene sire,
warisshed he is þat wil þe desire
ffrom þe fende sathan.   321
wel is hym þat suffren may
ffor þi loue niȝth oiþere day,
Peyne þat paie þee can.'   324

(28)

¶ whan noþing' nas hym bileued',
And he fer from his frendes to dreued',
his cloþes weren to rent'.   327
Amonge þe pouere in þe chirche hawȝe
he begged, & was her felawȝe,
And took' þat god hym sent'.   330
Almesse þat god hym ȝeue,
þe pouer þat wolde þere bileue
wiþ hym in present',   333

LAUD 622

He ȝaf þat haluendel & more,
And was hym-self of hungred sore,
And took' it in good entent'.   336

(29)

¶ Euery sonenday houseled he was,
And shryuen also of vche trespas
þat fel to any synne.   339
Michel he waked & litel he sleep,
Of þat he shulde his body wiþ kepe,
Litel hym com wiþinne.   342
ffrom þe tyme he took' his tourne
ffrom Rome, þere he was borne,
he was souȝth of his kynne   345
In alle cuntrees, in euery toun,
In chirche, in felde, vp & doun,
ffor nouȝth wolde þai blynne.   348

LAUD 622

That none of theyme shoullde thak hede,
And axed his met eorly and late,
With poremen att the mynster yate.
All the mete þat he myght gete,

COTTON

Bot euery day a melys mete   126
To pore men gaffe A. noone ryght,
he lefft hym sylffe none ouer nyght.
there dwellyd he xvij yere,   129
And lede his lyffe in thys manere;

COTTON

---

fforþi þe pore þat þer ware,
Alle þe betere miȝte fare
for heore Charite.   114
Alix, of al þat miȝte he gete,
nedliche bote he moste ete,
he ne held to his bi-houe;   117
To pore men þat wolde hit take,
he ȝaf hit for cristes sake,
þat sitteþ us alle aboue.   120

VERNON

ffor-þi þe pouere þat þer were,
Alle þe betere myȝtte fare
þoru here charite.   114
Alex, of þat he myȝtte gete
Nedliche bote þat him-self wolde ete
he ne held to his by-houe;   117
To pouere men þat wolde it take,
Al he ȝaf for godes sake,
þat is in heuene A-boue.   120

LAUD 108

Ouht' þat he spare myht
Be day, & eke be nyȟt,
his pore feren he delde.   210

LAUD 463

Al þat he spelye myȝte,
Be daye and ek' be nyȝte;
His pouere feren he delde.   210

TRINITY

(30)

¶ His kynrede com þere hym biside,
þat had ysouȝth hym fer & wide,
& ȝaf hym her Almesse,   351
As he satt amonge þe pouere,
In grete meschieft & stronge to couere,
ffor hunger in wrecchednesse.   354
Sore of hym þai gonnen rewe,
Stille he satt, & wel hem knewe,
Her names more & lesse.   357
Ychaunged was his faire hewe
þorouȝ reyn & wynde þat on hym blewe,
And oþer stronge destresse.   360

LAUD 622

(31)

¶ whan þai miȝtten nouȝth spede,
Ne hym of axen in no þede
Ne in no londe of take,   363
wiþ sorouȝ þai gradde, allas! allas!
And wenten to Rome, þe riȝth pas,
her sorouȝ miȝth nouȝth slake.   366
Alexius noþing þouȝth,
Bott on Iesu cristt he þouȝth,
And grete ioye he gan make   369
ffor he ne was nouȝth biknowe
Of his frendes heiȝe ne lowe,
His welþe gan a-wake.   372

LAUD 622

---

his Fader and hys modyr bothe,
Than he was to theyme Fvll lothe;
his fadyr made gret dole and sorowe,
Bothe on euen and on morowe.   134
'Alas!' he sayde, and wrong his honde,

COTTON

'Why is my sonne went owte of
   lond?
I wende haue hade of hym a knyght,
with me to stonde In all my ryght;
nowe ys he wente þat was my blysse,

COTTON

¶ Nou is Alix dwelled þore:
his fader atom sikeþ wel sore,
and seiþ, Allas! Allas!   123
His Moder wepeþ niht and day,
& seiþ, Allas! & weila-wey,
þat euere heo i-boren was.   126

VERNON

Nou is Alex dwelled þere;
his fader at hom seyetȝ sore,
& seyþ 'allas! allas!'   123
his moder wepuþ nyȝth & day
& seyþ 'allas & weylawey,
þat euere ȝhe born was.'   126

LAUD 108

Þo þe tiþing was y.-com
To þe fader of þe sone,
hou [he] was a-go,   213
him þouht his herte wold to-breke,
On word ne myht he speke,
for sorwe ne for wo.   216
Ofte he syȝte, & grente sore,
To tar his her, his lockes hore,
þe gode old man.   219
ȝerne he gradde godes ore,
þat he ne moste liue namor
to swoune he began.   222

LAUD 463

Þo þe tydynge was y-come
To þe fader of þe sone,
How he was a-go,   213
¶ Him þoȝte his herte wolde breke,
O lepy word he ne myȝte speke,
ffor sorwe and for wo;   216
Ofte he siȝte & grente sore,
To tar his shroud, his lokkes hore,
þe guode olde man.   219
ȝerne he gradde godis ore,
þat he ne moste lyue namore;
To swoȝeny he be-gan.   222

TRINITY

(32)

¶ Eufeniens seide in his mende,
'þe most wrecche fer oiþere hende
Certes now am I.   375
Conforte ne ioye ne may me come;
Now my childe is me bynome
My song is tourned to cry.   378
My wijf is barayne, & ek olde;
She ne may haue no childe for colde,
Oure heir al forto by.   381
In sorouȝ & care my lijf is diȝth,
ffor to dye it were my riȝth,
And hennes to party.'   384

LAUD 622

(33)

¶ wiþ þat his moder fel to grounde
And lay yswowen a longe stounde,
And roos vp al afrayed: 387
'My leue son, þat were so meke,
I ne woot where I shal þee seke,
þerefore I am dismayed.'   390
His moder ne miȝth lete sorouȝ,
Neiþer at euene ne at morowe,
In sawȝe as it is seide.   393
To hir chaumbre she went in hast,
And of hire bedd þe cloþes doun cast,
And siþen hem al to breyde,—   396

LAUD 622

I west hym neuer do man a mys.
Nowe haue I none of my lynage [lf 147]
That maye welde myn herytage.'
Than sayde his moder, and wepte full
        sore,   143

COTTON

'Noue shall I see my sonne no
        more;
I was full glade whan he was
        borne,
nowe ys all my Ioye forlorne.   146

COTTON

¶ His wyf wepeþ and makeþ hir mone,
& seiþ þat heo schal liuen alone
as turtul on þe treo.   129
Euermore with-outen Make,
Ioye and blisse heo wole forsake
til heo hire spouse i-seo.   132

VERNON

his wif wepþ & makeþ hire mone,
& þus [ȝhe] schal lyuen allone,
As turtle opon þe tre,   129
Euere-more wiþoute make;
Ioye & blisse ȝe wile for-sake,
Til ȝe hire spouse se.   132

LAUD 108

¶ his moder wiþ softe pas
went to bedde, & gradde 'allas
þat she was y.-bore.'   225
Nolde she neuere eft out-com,
þer' she weope for hir' sone,
þat she hadde lore.   228
All þat þer-inne were
// hem-self drouȝ be þe her',
& wrong' her' hond;   231
Besouȝte god, he shold hem ler',
To what lond he go wer',
& wher' he wer' astond.   234

LAUD 463

¶ His moder with wel softe pas
Wente to bedde, & gradde, 'allas,
þat hy was y-bore.'   225
Nolde hy neuere eft out-come,
Ac þere hy wep for here sone,
þat hy hadde for-lore.   228
Alle þat þer-ynne were,
Hem-selue drowe by þe here,
And wronge hare honde.   231
¶ Be-soȝte god þat sholde hem lere,
To what londe þat he were,
And whtre he were a-stonde.   234

TRINITY

¶ Ciclatounes þat weren of prijs,
Pelured wiþ Ermyne & wiþ grijs,
Alle she cast' away, 399
And wered cloþes symple & blake.
Litel she sleep, & mychel gan wake,
And fasted euery daye. 402

LAUD 622

'Lorde,' she seide, 'almiʒtty,
To þee & to þi moder mary
I make a vow, & saye, 405
þat I shal neuer hennes wende
Tyl Alexius come oiþer sende,
Oiþer I be roted in clay.' 408

LAUD 622

I haue hade robbys maney and fayre,
Nowe woll I next me were the ayre,
Tyll I maye some tydynges here

COTTON

of my sone that was so dere.' 150
than spake his wyffe, and wepte among.
'My leffe,' she sayde, 'was done wrong,

COTTON

Nou is fader, with dreri chere,
biddeþ his Men comen him nere,
as þei wolde haue heore mede. 135
He preʒeþ hem þat þei ben boun
to wenden & sechen his deore sone,
in eueriche a þeode; 138
þat ʒe ne dwelle for no þing,
er ʒe han herd sum god tiþing
wher þat he be. 141
Goþ nou forþ, and god ow spede,
þerfore i schal, so God me rede,
ʒiuen ou gold and ffe. 144

VERNON

Nou his fader wiþ dreri chere
He biddeþ his men him comen nere,
Als þei willen hauen þere mede, 135
& preyeþ hem þat þei ben boun,
To wende & sechen his dere sone
In euerich ilk a þede. 138
'þat ʒe ne dwelle for no þing,
Ar ʒe hauen herd sum tyding,
Where þat he be; 141
Goþ nou swyþe, & god ʒou spede!
þerfore I schal, so god me rede,
ʒiuen ʒou gold & fee.' 144

LAUD 108

---

his fader & his moder bo,
ffor her' sone wer' wo,
þat .I. ne may of telle. 237
fforto seke her' sone,
In which lond' he wer' becom
Men þei sent snell. 240
¶ It befel vpon a day,
þat þe men nom her' wey
forþ right be þe chirche; 243
þere her' lord' nyht' & day
Among' þe pore folk lay,
Cristes will to wirche. 246

LAUD 463

His fader & his moder bo,
ffor hare sone were ful wo,
þat ich ne may al telle. 237
ffor to sechen hare sone,
In what londe he were by-come,
ʒonge men he sente snelle. 240
¶ It by-fel opon a day, [leaf 75]
þat ʒonge men nome hare way
fforþ riʒt by þe cherche 243
þere hare lord nyʒt and day,
Among' þe pouere folk' lay,
Cristis wille to werche. 246

TRINITY

(35)

¶ Now mowen ȝee here pleynt' pitouse
Of Alexius trewe spouse,
Hou she made her mone ;   411
In gret' sorouȝ was hir entent',
Her here she drouȝ, her cloþes rent',
Grymly she gan grone.   414
   LAUD 622

'Al my ȝouþe & my solas,
Myne hope, is lorne, allas,
And my bidyng' alone. [leaf 23, back]
I. am boþe maiden & wijf',
I. noot' to whom telle my strijf',
I lyue as ankre in stone.   420
   LAUD 622

---

he toke me in my fadyrs bowre,
And brought me hydder with grete
 honouer.   154
   COTTON

And he has me nowe for-sakyng,
To Iesu cryst I wyll me takyne ; 156
   COTTON

¶ Now wende þei forþ Alix sekande,
vchone to diuerse lande,
ȝif þei miȝte him winne.   147
Summe of hem þorwh Godus grace,
comen in-to þat ilke place
þat Alix was Inne.   150
He sat in pore Mennes rowe,
þerfore þei couþe him not knowe,
þai ȝeuen him Charite.   153
He tok hit wiþ mylde mod,
and seide, 'Iesus, þat died on Rod,
lorde, i þonke þe.   156
   VERNON

Nou gon þei forþ Alex sekynd
In diuerse londes to here tyding,
ȝif þei him myȝtte wynne ;   147
Somme of hem, þoru godes grace,
Comen into þat ilke place
þer Alex was Inne.   150
he sat in pore mene rowe ;
þerfore couden he hym nat knowe ;
he ȝaf him charite ;   153
& he it tok wiþ milde mod,
And seyde 'Iesu, þat deyde on rod,
Louerd, I þanke þe !   156
   LAUD 108

---

he knew hem, & þei not him,
Of her' goed' þei ȝeuen him,
as it wolde falle.   249
he heried' god, & made him glad,
þat he for his loue hadde
Almes of his thralle.   252
Out' of þe bourgh þei went sone,
to her' lord' þei come
wiþ goed' spede.   255
Tiþinges none þei brouhte
Of his sone þat þei soughte,
In vnkouþe theode.   258
   LAUD 463

He hem knew, and hy noȝt him ;
Of hare guode hy ȝeue him,
As it wolde falle.   249
¶ He herede god, and made him glad,
þat he for his sone bad
Almesse of þralle.   252
Out of þe borgh hy wente sone
To here lord til þat þeȝ come
with wel guode spede.   255
Tydynges none hy ne broȝte
Of his sone, þat him soȝte,
In vncouþe þede.   258
   TRINITY

(36)

¶ 'Siþþe I ne haue to whom me mene,
Lijk' is my lijf' on to sene—
þat am wiþouten red— 423
þe turtel þat is for sorouȝ lene,
And tredeþ on no gras grene,
Siþen hire make is ded. 426

LAUD 622

Allas, hou shal I. ioye haue?
Oiþer hou shal I my-seluen saue
To lyue in maidenhede? 429
Me were leuer of hym a siȝth,
þan welde al þis londe riȝth
In lengþe & in brede.' 432

LAUD 622

Sorowe and morenyng may I well
  make,
As the turtell dothe withowten his
Ioyefull schall I neuer bee, [make.
Tyll I maye my leman see.' 160
hys Fader send bothe fer and vyde
Messengers on euery syde,
To seke his sonne where he was went,
Bothe Fer and nere where he was went.

COTTON

Sythen affter yt befell soo, 165
Of messengeres there com too,
Ryght to the Ryche Cete, [leaf 148]
There alex lywyd In pourte. 168
As they com In to a strete,
Alex com and shoulde hym mete;
Sone knewe he þeyme full welle,
And þey knewe hym neuer a dele.
lowde he spake vnder hys hoode,

COTTON

Lord, i-þonked be þou ay,
þat i haue beden þat ilke day,
þat i may for þi sake; 159
Of hem þat in myn owne lond,
serued me to fot and hond,
her Almus to take.' 162
Nou þis Men þat weren out-sent,
aȝein ham-ward þei hem went
to sire Eufemiane. 165
þei sworen alle bi heuene kyng
of Alix herde heo noþing,
as wide as þei hedden i-gone. 168
In eueri lond [þat] we han ben
we founde no mon þat him couþe sen,
þat to him couþe vs wisse. 171

VERNON

Louerd, i-her[i]d be þou ay!
þat i haue beden þat ilke day,
þat I may, for þi sake, 159
Of hem þat in myn owene lond
Serueden me to fot & hond
Here Almesse forto take.' 162
Nou þese men þat were out-sent,
aȝen homward þei ben I-went
To sire eufemian. 165
þei swore to him be heuene king:
Of Alex herde þei no tyding,
As wyde as þei hadde gan. 168
'In eche a lond þan haue we be,
We ne founden no man þat couþe
þat to him coude vs wisse.' [him se,

LAUD 108

¶ Þo þis ȝongman woned hadd
In þe toun as a pore ladde
ȝeres seuentene, 261
God wolde his care wende,
& to his fader hous him send,
to bring' him out of teone. 264

LAUD 463

¶ Þo þis ȝonge man y-woned hadde
In toune as a pouere ladde,
ȝeres seuentene, 261
God self wolde his care wende,
And to his fader him sende,
And bringe him of tene. 264

TRINITY

ST. ALEXIUS DWELLS IN POVERTY 17 YEARS.

(37)

¶ She roos vp erlich a morowe,	þe lefdy was wel apaied
And to his moder she went in sorouȝ	whan she had þus yseied,
ffor loue of hire spouse, 435	þat was so preciouse. 441
And praied hir þat she most duelle	And at oo bed & oo cloþing,
wiþ hir, þat sorouȝful pleynt to telle,	Seuentene ȝer was her duellyng
þat strong was and greuouse. 438	Boþe in one house. 444
LAUD 622	LAUD 622

'For goddes lowe do me som goode;'	hate gewyn me of theyre cheryte.'
Theye gaffe hym of theyre money,	Alex dwellyd styll there
For goddes lowe there in the waye.	Fully xlij yere and more. 184
whan Alex sawe þeye knwe hym nought, 177	To chyrche he went euery daye, his goode bedeyes there for to saye;
he thanked god in all hys thought.	In to that chyrche, with owtyn fayle,
'lorde,' he sayde, 'I thank the	Was an Images of fayre entayele,
the grace þat thowe hast sent me;	Of owre lady þat is so Free, 189
Myne owne men that shoullde bee,	With here sonne wppon here knee;
COTTON	COTTON

"Nou, allas! þat i was boren;	'Allas, he seyde, þat he was born!
boþe haue i nou forloren	boþe¹ haue I nou for-lorn [¹ boþo MS.]
mi Ioye and my blisse." 174	Mi ioye & ek my blisse.' 174
¶ In þis tale wol we non dwelle,	In þis tale wille we nat dwelle,
of Alix wol we nou telle,	Bote of Alex wile we telle,
þat riche pore mon. 177	þat riche pore man. 177
Alix was pore Monnes fere	Alex was pouere mannes fere
fulle seuentene ȝere,	ffulli seuentene ȝere,
fro þat he bi-gon, 180	fro þat he bi-gan, 180
Sittinge in a chirche-ȝerde,	Syttynde in a churche-ȝerd,
among pore men an herde,	Amonges oþere men an herd
in a simple wede. 183	In a simple wede. 183
An ymage in þat chirche stoode	An ymage in þat cherche stod,
of his Modur þat died on rode,	Of his moder þat deyde on rood
for ur alre nede. 186	ffor oure alþres nede. 186
VERNON	LAUD 108

It befel in a nyght	It by-fel in one nyȝt
þat þe mone shoñ bright,	þe mone shon swyþe bryȝt,
þe belleward him wend. 267	þe belward hym by-wende. 267
þe leme of heueñ he sey aliht,	¶ þe leome of heuene he seȝ a liȝt,
& stonde vpe godes knyght,	And stonde ope godis knyȝt,
þat al þe chirche a-tende. 270	þat al þe cherche attende. 270
LAUD 463	TRINITY

(38)

¶ Lordynges, ȝee þat willeþ lere,
a faire miracle ȝee mowen here :
Bifore þat self ymage,   447
þere þat Alexius sate
wiþ pouere men in þe gate
As a pouere page,   450
þe ymage, þat aungels gonne wirche,
Spaak' to þe serieauntz of þe chirche
þere she stood on þe stage,   453
And hete hem alle wiþouten lettynge
Goddes sergeaunt to chirche brynge
wiþouten any outrage.   456

LAUD 622

(39)

¶ 'He is riȝth stedfast of lijf';
His werkes shullen ben made rijf'
Ouer al fer & neere.   459
þe holy gost wiþinne hym rest ;
Charite sitteþ in his breest,
Brennande as fyre.   462
Longe in pouerte his lijf he haþ led ;
He ne com neuere in no bed'
þise seuentene ȝere ;   465
His holy lijf, bot god alone,
Ne woot non in þis werldes wone ;
To seintȝ he may be pere.'   468

LAUD 622

That Images spake, þat was so bryght,
to the sexteyene vppon a nyght. 192
¹'Take,' sche sayde, 'my seruante
    swythe,   [¹ leaf 148, back]

COTTON

he hathe me seruyd all hys lyeffe ;
Full offte he wolle to me lowthe,
hit is no ryght þat he is withowte.'
'lady,' he sayde, 'I knowe hym nought,

COTTON

¶ Atte seuentene ȝeres ende
spac and seide wordus hende
þat ymage of tre,   189
To þe wardein of þe chirche,
& seide, "wardein, if þou worche
eny-þing for me,   192
"ffecche þou in mi sones nom,
for seuentene ȝer hit is gon
þat he haþ ben þer-oute.   195
I warne þe witerli
to dwelle her-in he is worþi,
þer-of haue þou no doute ;   198
"He haþ serued heuene briȝt,
þe holi gost in him is liht,
& ȝiueþ him miȝt and grace,   201

VERNON

At þe seuentene ȝeres ende,
Spak & seyde wordes hende,
þat ymage of tre,   189
To þe wardeyn of þe churche,
& seyde : 'wardeyn, ȝif þou werche
Enyþing for me,   192
ffecche þou In my sones man,
ffor seuentene ȝer it is i-gan
þat he haþ ben þer-oute ;   195
I þe warne wyterly,
To duelle her-inne he is worþi ;
Whar-of ne haue no doute.   198
he haþ deserued heuene bryȝth,
þe holy gost is in him lyȝth
& ȝiuen him myȝtte & grace,   201

LAUD 108

---

¹¶ Sone at morwe whan it was day,
þat he be þis man say,   [¹ leaf 117]
wide he it tolde.   273

LAUD 463

Sone amorwe, so it was day,
þat he by þis manne i-say,
Wyde he it tolde.   273

TRINITY

(40)

¶ þe sergeauntz lepen out in hast,
As men þat weren sore agast,
And ful of grete drede 471
Of þe ymage þat to hem spak
Of goddes sergeaunt wiþouten lak
þat sat in beggers wede. 474
wyde aboute þai hym souȝth,
And ȝut founden þai hym nouȝth
Amonge þe pouere felawrede; 477
And whan þai nouȝth hym fynde miȝth,
To þat ymage onon riȝth
Hastilich þai ȝede, 480

LAUD 622

(41)

¶ To þat Maryole wiþ teres clere,
And bisouȝth hir on þis manere,
'þat she sent hem grace 483
Goddes man hou þai shulden knowe,
þat had ben heiȝe & bare hym lowe,
And where he sat in place.' 486
þe ymage spaak ofte wordes newe,
'I ȝou hote, sergeauntȝ trewe,
Aȝein[ward] þat ȝee pace; 489
Amonge þe pouere he sitteþ, to-tore
Boþe bihynde & bifore,
wiþ a lene face.' 492

LAUD 622

Nor I wott neuer where he schull be
   sought.' 198
She sayde, 'he sitteþe eorly and late
Withowtyn att the mynster yate.'

COTTON

Anon he owte of his slepe brayde,
And thought what þe Image sayde.
And forthe went the sextayne, 203
And fownde alex knelyng In þe Rayne.

COTTON

þat his preȝere, with milde steuene,
is swete & god & heiȝ in heuene
bi-fore mi sone face." 204
¶ þenne seide þe wardeyn, 'ladi,'
he seide, 'i wolde fayn, & i
wuste whulche.' 207
'Go out faste as þou maiȝt go,
þou fyndest þer on & no mo,
bring him in þat ilche.' 210
þe wardein wente him out ful ȝare,
he fond him redi sittinge þare,
he brouȝte him in ful sone. 213
He seide, 'sire, ȝif hit be þi wille,
þou art welcome nou vs tille,
here-in schaltou wone. 216

VERNON

þat his preyer wiþ milde stephene
Is good & swete & mylde in heuene
Byfore my sones face.' 204
þanne ansuerede þe wardeyn
& seyde: 'lauedi, I wille ful fayn,
and I wiste wilk.' [leaf 235] 207
'Go owt so swiþe so þou mayst go,
þou ne fyndest þer no mo,
Bryng him [in] þat ilk!' 210
þe wardeyn wente him out ful ȝare,
he fond [him] redy sittinde þere,
he brougthe him In ful sone; 213
And [seyde]: 'sire, ȝif it be þi wille,
þou art welcome vs vntille,
Her-Inne schaltou wone; 216

LAUD 108

To þe chirche þei gonne teo
þilk holy man to seo,
Boþe ȝong & olde. 276

LAUD 463

To þe cherche hy gonne teo,
þe holy man for to seo,
Boþe ȝonge and olde. 276

TRINITY

(42)

¶ þe sergeauntȝ stirten out' skeet',
þai founden hym, & kisten his feet',
And mercy þai hym cryde, 495
And ledden hym in-to holy chirche,
Goddes werkes forto wirche,
þereinne to abide. 498
Of þe gode mannes loos
þe miracle & þe cry aroos
Ouere al in vche syde; 501
Michel poeple þider ran,
Of þe miracles þat herden þan,
Of cuntrees fer & wyde; 504

LAUD 622

(43)

¶ And worschiped hym in word & dede,
Alle þat miȝtten in lengþe & brede;
And duden hym gret honoure, 507
And beden hym, boþe day & niȝth,
He bere her erande to god almiȝth
þat is oure saueoure. 510
þo was Alexius swiþe woo
ffor þat he was honoured soo,
And made grete doloure; 513
For swiche honoure & swiche glorie,
As it is writen in his storye,
He ne loued in toun ne toure. 516

LAUD 622

Fayne was he that he hym founde,
A-non he toke hym vpe be þe hande.
'A-ryse,' he sayde, 'my leve and dere,
hit ys no ryght þat thowe sitt here.

COTTON

Com,' he sayde, 'my lady bade,
And there of mayst þou be glade.'
All that hard this tydynges, 211
Theye worshippyd Iesu, hewyn kyng.

COTTON

'I was out aftur þe sent,
þorwh vr ladies comaundement,
þe in forte take; 219
with muchel honour schaltou haue
alle þing þat þou wolt craue,
for þat ladies sake.' 222
¶ þenne þis word bi-gon to springe,
& of him was gret spekynge,
for his holynesse. 225
þerfore he þouȝte forte wende,
to anoþur lond forte lende,
þer me kneuȝ him lesse. 228

VERNON

I was out after þe i-sent,
þoru our lauedies comandement,[1]
þe in forto take. [1 MS. comandememeut]
Mechul honur schaltou haue,
& alle þing þat þou wilt craue,
ffor þat lauedies sake.' 222
Whan þis word be-gan to springe,
þat of him was a gret spekyngge
ffor his holinesse, 225
Sone he þoutthe forto wende,
To oþer londe forto lende,
þere men him knewe lesse. 228

LAUD 108

¶ þis holy man turned his thought,
worshipe of men kepte he nouȝt',
þat is frakel atte ende. 279
Out of bourgh he went' anon,
to þe watur he com gon,
þer-ouer he moste wende. 282

LAUD 463

¶ þis holy man turnde his poȝt,
Herynge of man ne kepte he noȝt,
þat frel is atte ende. 279
Out of þe borgh he wente anon,
To a water til þat he com,
þer-ouer he moste wende. 282

TRINITY

(44)

¶ ffor þat his meryte wolde slake
þat he shulde of god take,
þerfore it liked hym ille. 519
werldes honoure forto flee,
Al by niȝth, in pryuete,
He stale away ful stille 522
In-to þe londe of Galys.
To seint Iames chirche I-wys
he com wiþ gode wille, 525
And þere he sete amonge pouere men,
And beged his mete in þe fen, [leaf 24]
his penaunce to fulfille. 528

LAUD 622

(45)

¶ þoo he had þere twelfmonþe ysete
wiþ pouere Men, & begged his mete,
His fadres sergeauntȝ come 531
And souȝtten hym forsoþe I-wys
In pilerynage atᵗ Galys,
To bryngen hym to Rome. 534
And whan Alexius hem gan see,
Stillelich he gan flee,
As man of riȝt wisdome: 537
In-to thars he þouȝth fare,
And atᵗ þe Royn he fonde ȝare
A shippe þat was al tome, 540

LAUD 622

Whan Alex sawe hit schulde be ryffe,
hys penance and hys holy lyffe, 214
here kepte he to haue mede,
In this worllde for his goode deede;

COTTON

Bytt stylly he yeede a waye [leaf 149]
In to a-nodr dyuers contre. 218
To þe se he cam in þat entente,
In to spreusse he wolde haue wente;

COTTON

þer wolde he no lengor beo:
monnus honour forte fle,
fro þat stude he wente 231
In-to Laodiciane,
forþ þe riȝte wey a-none,
as Iesu crist him sente. 234
In-to a-noþur lond he þouȝt,
godus wille til he hedde wrouȝt,
þer nomon hed him knowe. 237
Assone as he was in þe se,
forte wende þer he wolde beo,
þe wynd bi-gon to blowe; 240

VERNON

þere ne wolde he lengere be,
Mannes honur forto fle,
ffro þat stede he wende 231
Anon to laodician
fforþ þe ryȝtte wey anon,
Als iesu crist him sende. 234
To A-noþer lond he þout,
Godes wille to han I-wrouth,
þer noman ne hadde him knowe. 237
Als swiþe as he was in þe se
fforto wende þer he wolde be,
þe wynd be-gan to blowe. 240

LAUD 108

// Into þe shipe he went a nyȝht,
Elles-whare þei hadde tyght
Into vnkouþe londe. 285
þei wentᵗ fairʼ swiþe ryghtᵗ,
& sone at morwe þo it was lyht
At Rome þei gonne astonde. 288

LAUD 463

In-to þe schip he wente anyȝt,
ffor elles-whar he hadde i-dyȝt
In-to vncouþe londe. 285
¶ He wende fare swiþe riȝt,
Ac sone amorwe þo it was liȝt,
At Rome hy gonne a-stonde. 288

TRINITY

(46)

¶ And Pilgrymes gret' plente
þat wolden passen ouer þe Cee,
To tars þat wolden ȝare.   543
He bad þe shipman, for goddes loue
þat is in heuene vs aboue,
he most wiþ hem fare.   546
Grete grucchyng' þai alle made;
Alexius fer & ner gan wade,
ffor nouȝth wolde he spare;   549
Euere he cried loude & shille,
Til þai graunted hym his wille,
þoo was he out' of care.   552

(47)

¶ þai drowen vp seil, þe wynde was
And saileden ouer þe salt' flood, [good',
þe weder was at her wille;   555
vntil, þe þrid dayes ende,
Swiche a storme Iesus gan sende,
þat alle hem liked ille.   558

LAUD 622

þai wenden wel haue went to tars;
þe wynde was gret, & noþing skars,
þonder dyned shille;   561
ffor liȝttynges grete, & þonder blast',
wel sore þe poeple was agast',
þai grete & groned grille.   564

(48)

¶ þe wynde hem droof, forsoþe to
In-to þe londe of Romeyne, [seyne,
þere Alexius was borne;   567
þoo was þe poeple in wel more care,
ffor þat þai were aryued þare,
þan þai wereṅ er biforne;   570
ffor þat tyme were þe folk' of Rome
þe mest shrewen of cristendome
wiþouten oþes ysworne.   573
ffor pilgrymes þat aryueden þere,
her catel þat þai wiþ hem bere,
On hast was forlorne.   576

LAUD 622

---

byt there com A storme of wynde &
  rayne,[1]   [1 MS. raynde]   221
And droffe þe shipe home a
  gayne,

COTTON   .

That In a lytyll stonde they come
Ryght to þe cyte of rome.   224
Alex sayde þan with sympyll cher,
'Alas!' he sayde, 'wat do we here?

COTTON

þe wynt bi-gon þe schip to driue,
til þei bi-gonne to aryue,
as hit was godus wille,   243
In rome, þer he was fed & boren,
þer his woninge was bi-foren,
of al him þhuȝte hit ille.   246

VERNON

þe wynd be-gan þe schip to dryue
Til þat he be-gonne to Aryue,
Als it was godes wille,   243
In rome þer he was fed & born,
þer his wonyng was be-forn,
þei al him þoute ille.   246

LAUD 108

¶ þo he to londe come
Into þe toun he moste rome,
his liflode to wynne.   291

LAUD 463

þo he in-to þe lond com,
In-to þe toune he moste gon,
His lyflode to wynne.   291

TRINITY

(49)

¶ Riȝth so bifel by þoo dawes
By Alexius & his felawes.
Of␣souruȝ was her speche; 579
Also sumtyme bifel a cas,
þoo god almiȝtty bad Ionas
To Nyniue gon & preche; 582
Ionas wist wel her wille,
þe folkͭ of niniue weren ille
And wicked for to teche; 585
Away Ionas wolde haue ystole
ffrom goddes hestͭ, & han hym hole;
Akͭ sone hym fel a wreche. 588

(50)

¶ Ionas wende god bigile,
And wolde haue went to anoþer yle
In þe grikkissh Cee; 591
he gan to shippen atte Ryuage;
wynde aroos wiþ wood rage,
þat souruȝ it was to see. 594

LAUD 622

ffyue dayes euere iliche it lestͭ
wiþ souruȝ & care, her tempestͭ,
þat seyl ne miȝth þere be. 597
þan seide þe maister 'forsoþe Iwys
Sum cursed Man amonges vs is,
þat wel witen mowe we. 600

(51)

¶ 'we willeþ caste amonges vs alle,
Lottͭ, on whom it may bifalle,
And ouere bordͭ he shal be castͭ.' 603
And whan þe prophete herde þis,
He þouȝth he had ydon amys,
And was sore agastͭ. 606
þries þai beren aboute þat lotͭ,
Ac on Ionas fel vche grotͭ,
þe first and þe lastͭ. 609
þe maister hym þrew ouere bordͭ;
A whal hym swalewe at oo wordͭ
ffor oo morsel in hastͭ; 612

LAUD 622

Myght hitt haue bene afftter me,
here woHde I nought haue I-bee;
Butt gode woHde hit myght befaH
I myght be in my fadris hauH, 230

COTTON

So that I myght vnknowen be
of hym and of his meyny.'

COTTON

---

whon he sauȝ non oþur won,
he bi-þouȝte him sone Anon,
wher him was best to be. 249
To him-self he seide and þouȝt,
'siþen þat Iesu haþ me brouȝt
in-to þis Cite, 252

VERNON

Whan he saw non oþer won,
he be-þoutte him sone anon,
Whare him was best to be; 249
To him-sulf he seyde & þouȝth:
'Siþen Iesus me haþ hider i-brouȝth
In-to þis cite, 252

LAUD 108

As he wentͭ þoruh þe strete,
his oune fader he gan mete,
As he com fro his inne. 294

LAUD 463

As he wente þorgh þe strete,
His owene fader he gan mete,
As he com fram his ynne. 294

TRINITY

(52)

¶ And þere he dwelled forsoþe apliȝth
þre dayes fulle & þre niȝth,
ffor Ionas was vntrewe ; 615
And att þe þre dayes ende,
Swiche grace god gan sende,
þe Cee to londe hym þrewe. 618
whan þe whal was comen to londe,
þerto was many mannes honde
On hym forto hewe ; 621
And whan þe whal was to-cleued,
Ionas pylte vp his heued,
And gan his body shewe. 624
      LAUD 622

(53)

¶ vp he roos, þe folk^t to teche,
And goddes wordes he gan preche,
And lered hem her lefnesse, 627
And made hem wynne goddes loue,
To wonen wiþ hym in heuene aboue,
þe poeple more and lesse. 630
¶ Riȝth so Alexius had yment^t
To Tars forto haue ywent^t ;
Ac god hym sent destresse, 633
And made hym to Rome wende,
To wonen þere among his frende,
holy wryt bereþ witnesse. 636
      LAUD 622

Forthe he vent vpe be a strete,
many a man there gan mete ; 234
But there was no man þat hym knwe,
      COTTON

So was he lene and blake of hewe.
There come his fader hyme agayne,
      COTTON

' I con no beter red of alle,
bote go to my fader halle,
in pore mennes route. 255
I may sitte vppon þe rowe ;
þer nis no mon schal me knowe,
so longe ichaue ben oute. 258
¶ Vppon a day Eufemiane
fro his paleis was he gane,
and ham-ward he eode, 261
with muche folk þat wel was diȝt,
boþe swein, [&] knaue, & kniȝt,
þat gode weren at nede. 264
      VERNON

I ne can no betere red of alle,
Bote gon to my faderes halle
In pore mannes rowte, 255
I may sitte in þe rowe,
þer nis no man þat me schal knowe :
So longe Ich haue ben oute.' 258
Vpon a day sire Eufemian
ffro þe paleys was he gan,
And homward he ȝede, 261
Wiþ mikel folk þat wel waren dyȝth,
Boþe knaue sweyn & knyth,
þat gode were in nede. 264
      LAUD 108

// þo þe sone his fader mette,
Mildeliche he him grette,
And bad him som gode. 297
þe godeman sone herd his bone,
for al his blod gan menge sone
vpon his oune fode. 300
      LAUD 463

¶ þo þe sone his fader mette,
Wel myldeliche he him grette,
And bad him of his guode. 297
þe guode man grantede his bone,
ffor al his blod gan menge sone
Ope his owene fode. 300
      TRINITY

(54)

¹¶ whan Alexius was to londe ygon,
Seyl þai drouȝen vp onon, [¹leaf 24, back]
And wenten in þe Cee,   639
Al to thars till þai come
ffro þe wicked londe of Rome,
And maden solempnite.   642
Alexius com in-to his owe,
And of his frendes was he nouȝth
ffor so naked was he;   [knowe,
And als a straunge man he wentᵗ
To his fader wiþ gode ententᵗ,
And seide to hym par charite,   648

LAUD 622

(55)

¶ 'Eufeniens, goddes frende,
þou artᵗ holden good & hende,
Alesed of gret Almesse!   651
ffor his loue þat was ybete,
And for vs suffred woundes grete,
helpe me in þis destresse,   654
ffor I ne can to no Man gon
Mete to crauen, botᵗ þee on,
No herberewe more ne lesse;   657
Make of me þi bede-man!
And by hym þat þis werlde wan,
þou miȝth haue heuene blis;   660

LAUD 622

With mayny a knyght and many a
   swane,   238
Than com with hym on ylke a syde;

COTTON

Alex stode stelle theyme to a-byde.
'Syr,' he sayde, 'for goddes sake
Wyll yee thys porman In thake?

COTTON

¶ Alix þouȝte he wolde him mete,
& ron faste bi þe strete,
til þat he him mette.   267
whon he sauȝ þat he was neiȝ,
with a vois [boþ] loude & heiȝ,
Eufemian his fader he grette,   270
And seide with a milde steuene,
'sire, for godus loue of heuene,
haue merci of me.   273
Icham a pilgrim pore & naked,
þat haþ gret defaute ymaket,
sire, as ȝe mowe se.   276

VERNON

Alex þoute he wolde him mete;
& ran forþ faste be þe strete
Vn-til þat he him mette;   267
Whan he say þat [he] was ney,
Wiþ a voys boþe loud & hey,
Sire Eufemian he grette,   270
& seyde wiþ a mylde stephene:
'Sire, for godes loue of heuene
haue merci on me!   273
Ich am a pilgrym pore & nakud,
þat gret defaute haþ I-maked,
Sire, as ȝe may I-se.   276

LAUD 108

¶ Ȝet spak þis holy man
To his fader Eufemyan,
wiþ mylde mode: 303
'þat goedᵗ þat þou þenkestᵗ do me,
Iesu Cristᵗ it ȝelde þe,
þat diede on þe Rode;   306

LAUD 463

ffor ȝut him spakᵗ þe holy man
To his fader Eufemian,
With wel mylde mode: 303
¶ 'þat guod þat þou þenkest do me,
Iesu crist it ȝelde þe,
þat deyde on þe rode.   306

TRINITY

(56)

¶ 'ȝiue me þe cromwes of þi table,—
þan doostou dedes merciable,—
And herberewe in þine house; 663
And of Alexius, þi son so fre,
Afterward I shal telle þee,
þat þou helde preciouse: 666
þan shaltou be day & niȝth
Glad, whan þou hym seest wiþ siȝth,
And ek' þi trewe spouse.' 669
Eufeniens ansuered þoo,
'I graunt wel þat it be so.
þine bedes ȝif þou wilt' ouse.' 672

LAUD 622

(57)

¶ To a Man he hym bitook',
þat seke Men couþe wel look',
Nouȝth as a Man of task'; 675
To kepe þat Man he bad hym þink',
And brynge hym boþe mete & drynk'
whan he wolde ask'. 678
'ȝif god wil, my creatoure,
He shal be kepte wiþ honoure,
His peynes forto lask', 681
To seien his bedes, & bidde for me
To veray god in trinite,
fforto he be roted to ask'.' 684

LAUD 622

---

for his lowe þat dyed on Roode, [lf 149, back]
Gywe me clethe and manys foode;
and for his lowe þat went for the,

COTTON

God sende þe grace hym for to see.'
This ryche man with stode þan, 247
And callyd one of his owne men,

COTTON

Receiue me in-to þin halle, [lf 44, col. 2]
þer þi pore men aren alle;
and graunte me þe mete, 279
And i schal preȝe niȝt and day
for þi sone þat is a-way,
þat Iesu crist him gete, 282
And grante þe, for his woundes fyue,
þat þou mai seo him ȝit a-lyue
þat was þin herte blisse; 285
And þe, sire, withoute strif,
Ioye of him in soule lyf,
crist þe to him wisse.' 288

VERNON

'Resceyue me into þin halle,
þere þine pore men ben alle,
& graunte me þe mete! 279
And I schal preye nyȝth & day
for þi sone þat is awey,
þat Iesu crist him þe gete, 282
'& grante þe, for his wondes fiue,
þat þou myttest him se in þine lyue,
þat was þin herte blisse, 285
&, sire, to habbe wiþoute strif
Ioye of him in soule & lif,
Crist þe til him wisse.' 288

LAUD 108

---

ffor if it is in þi mode
þat þou hast any fode,
In vnkouþe londe, 309
Crist' .I. beseke, par charite,
þat he wile to him seo
wher' he beo astonde.' 312

LAUD 463

ffor ȝif it is in þyne mode,
þat þou hauest eny fode,
In vncouþe londe, 309
Crist ich by-seche par charite,
þat he wel to him by se,
Wher þat he be a-stonde.' 312

TRINITY

ST. ALEXIUS IS KINDLY TREATED BY HIS PARENTS.   51

(58)

¶ Eufeniens bad he shulde be
þere þat he miȝth hym ysee
late and erly;   687
In þe halle he shulde be layd,
was þere non þat it wiþsayd,
Bot graunted hastyly;   690
þai loued hym more þan any man.
To kepe hym wel, he hete hem þan,
And wisten neuer why   693
His wijf hym loued at herte dere;
wel wolde she þat he serued were,
And mychel was hym by.   696

LAUD 622

(59)

¶ wiþouten any grucchyng word,
Mete þat was vpon hire bord
þai senten hym to almesse,   699
Riȝth of her owen dissh,
were it flessh oiþer fissh,
while he was in destresse;   702
þus was þe pilegryme yserued þan.
who he was, wist noman,
Gret was his þolemodenesse;   705
ffor ȝif his moder oiþer his wijf
hadden ywist Alexius lijf,
It had ben her gladnesse.   708

LAUD 622

And gaffe hym mete an dr[i]nk bothe,
And with pore men hym to clothe.
There dwellyd alex wythem alle,

COTTON

Sewentene yere in his Faders hall;
There was no man, hye ne llawe,
yong ne owlde, þat hym myght knowe;

COTTON

¶ þenne Eufemian with-stod,
and grantede wiþ a milde mod
þat pore mon his bone.   291
He grantede him forte cloþe and feede,
and bad his men heo scholden him lede
to his hous al sone.   294
He grantede him, as i ou telle,
an hous al-one þer-in to dwelle,
wiþ-outen eny fere;   297
And a mon þat scholde him gete,
& bringe him boþe drinke and mete,
whon þat mester were.   300

VERNON

þanne eufemian þer wiþstod,
& grantede him wiþ milde mod,
þe pore man his bone;   291
he grantede him to cloþe & fede,
& bad his men he scholde him lede
To his hous as sone;   294
And grauntede him, as [I] ȝou telle,
An hous allone þer-in to dwelle
Wiþ-outen eny fere;   297
& a man þat scholde him gete
And bringe him boþe drynk & mete,
Whan þat mester were.   300

LAUD 108

¶ þo he spak of his sone,
þe godeman, as it was his wone,
Gan to sike sore.   315
his herte fel cold so stone,
þe teres fellen to his tone,
Ouer his berd hore.   318

LAUD 463

¶ So sone so he spak of his sone,
þe guode man, as was his wone,
Gan to sike sore.   315
His herte fel so cold so ston,
þe teres felle to his ton,
Ouer his berd hore.

TRINITY

(60)
¶ wiþ hym þai speken, & hym seiȝen
wiþ her mouþe & wiþ her eiȝen,
ffader & moder & wijfᵗ;   711
Nouȝth for þan non hym knew,
Noiþer by hide ne by hew;
Al chaunged was his lijfᵗ.   714
His fader he seiȝ often grete,
And his moder teres lete
ffourty siþes & fyue.   717

LAUD 622

yuel miȝth hym liken þat seiȝ þis;
his martirdom was strongᵗ I-wys,
Of sorouȝ & paynes ryue.   720
(61)
¶ Alexius in al wise
Dude to god his seruise
wiþ stedfast wille in hertᵗ,   723
In fastyngᵗ, & in orisouns,
In many manere deuociouns
Of peynes þat weren smertᵗ.   726

LAUD 622

---

his owne men for rebaundrye   255
dyd hym manye a welonye.

COTTON

They hylde water wppon hys
hede,

COTTON

¶ Nou Alix, as ȝe han [i]herd,
is dwelled in his fader ȝerd,
as a pore mon;   303
In preȝere, wakynge, and fastinge,
he seruede Iesu, heuene kynge,
in al þat he con.   306
Seruauns þat were proude and ȝinge,
þei driuen him ofte to skorninge,
as heo eoden vp and doun;   309
And ofte-siþes broþ of fissches,
& watur þat þei wosschen in dissches,
heo casten vpon his croun.   312

VERNON

Nou Alex, As ȝe habbeþ i-herd,
Is dweld in his fader ȝerd
As a pore man.   303
In preyere of fasting & waking,
he seruede Iesu, heuene kyng,
In al þat he can.   306
Seruantȝ þat were proute & ȝungge,
him dryuen ofte to heþingge,
As he ȝede vp & doun;   309
& ofte-siþes, broþ of ffissches,
& water, as he wessch here dissches,
þei caste vp-on his croun.   312

LAUD 108

¶ To his hous þe pore he broughte,
And a ȝong man him betaughte
to serue him to queme.   321
þere he woned day & nyȝht,
& serued god wiþ al his myht,
ȝeres ȝette seuentene.   324
// Somme þat of þe in were
þe holymannes cloþes tere,
þere he lay in his bedde;   327
Ofte þei drowe be þe here,
& of brohtᵗ & watur cler
þei caste in his nebbe.   330

LAUD 463

¹To his house þe pouere he broȝte;
One ȝonge man him be-toȝte
To seruy him to queme.   321
¶ þere he wonede day and nyȝt,
And seruede god with al his myȝt,
ȝeres ȝut seuentene. [¹ leaf 75, back]   324
Some of þo þer-ynne were
þe holy mannes clothes tere,
þere hy leȝe on his bedde.   327
Ofte hy drowe him by þe here,
And of water and of broþ him bere,
And caste in his nebbe.   330

TRINITY

And al was forto wynne heuene;
To here Aungels wiþ mylde steuene,
he suffred þis pouert' 729
ffulle seuentene ȝer;
he wered breech maked of her,
And al swiche was his shert'. 732
(62)
¶ Sergeauntz, þat þere-inne were,
Ofte siþes gramed hym þere,
And despised hym fast'. 735

LAUD 622

þe wasshyng' of her vessel
þai cast on hym euerydel,
þat was swiþe vnwrast'; 738
And cleped hym shrewe ypo-
crite,
And ofte-tymes gonne hym smyte
Vnder þe cheke in hast': 741
Ac Alexius was of god fulfild,
In gode penaunce he it helde,
And þanked hem at þe last'. 744

LAUD 622

And gaff hym þat was in the dyche
   levyd;

COTTON

But euer he hylde hym stylle, 259
And Alle he suffyrde with goode wyll.

COTTON

Of al þe schome þat þei him wrouȝte,
he þonked Iesu þat him bouȝte,
& ȝaf him miȝt þer-to. 315
He was meke in alle þing,
þer-of miȝte no mon him bring,
for nouȝt þat þei couþe do. 318
¶ Alix dwelled þere stille,
as hit was Iesus cristes wille,
seuentene ȝere 321
In his owne fader Inne;
kneuȝ him non of al his kunne,
neiþer fer ne nere. 324

VERNON

[1] Of al þe schame þat þei him wrouȝthe,
He þonkede Iesu, þat him bouthe,
& ȝaf him myȝtte þerto; [¹ leaf 235, back]
He was þolemod in alle þinge,
þer-out ne myȝtte no man him bringe,
ffor nowth þei couden do. 318
þere dwelde Alex stille,
As it was Iesu cristes wille,
Seuentene ȝer; 321
In his owene faderes In,
kneu him non of al his kyn,
Neyþer fer ne ner. 324

LAUD 108

// Ofte þei him bete & buste,
þat þe lord þer-of niste,
þese wikkede fode. 333
þei clepeden him waste bred,
& wissheden þat he wer' ded,
y.-wis þei wer' wode. 336
¶ Al þe shame þat he drey,
þe while he was his fader ney,
he þolede with mylde mode. 339
And ofte to god he gan grede,
þat he forȝaf' her' misdede,
& bringe hem to gode. 342

LAUD 463

¶ Ofte hy him bete and burste,
þat þe lord þer-of nuste,
þo vnlede fode. 333
þeȝ clepude him 'waste bred,'
And weste þat he wer' ded;
I-wis hy wer' wode. 336
Al þe shame þat he dreȝ,
þe whyle he wonede his fader neȝ,
He þolede with mylde mode. 339
¶ And ofte to god he gan grede,
þat he for-ȝeue hem hare mysdede,
And broȝte hem to guode. 342

TRINITY

(63)

¶ Alexius, þat was goddes kniȝth,
ffor penaunce þat was on hym liȝth,
Almest his lijf was lorne. [leaf 25] 747
Wel he seiȝ, þorouȝ deþes lawȝes,
þat he drouȝ to his endyng͛ dawȝes,
ffor deþ com hym biforne. 750
His sergeaunt he cleped sone,
And for his loue, bad hym a bone,
þat bare þe crovne of þorne, 753
To fecche hym enk͛ & parchemyne,
fforto write in latyne
His lijf͛ sippe he was borne. 756

(64)

¶ His sergeaunt was glad & bliþe ;
Enk͛ & parchemyn also swiþe
He fette, & hym bitook͛ ; 759

LAUD 622

Alexius þo write bigan ;
Ak͛ þere was non bifore þan
þat wist he couþe in book͛. 762
þere-inne he wroot oord͛ & ende,
Hou he fro his wijf gan wende,
And al his kyn forsook͛ ; 765
And hou Alex at his partyng͛,
whan he took͛ his wijf þe ryng͛,
hou rewly she gan look͛ ; 768

(65)

¶ And hou in pilerynage he ȝede,
In hunger, in þorst, in pouere wede,
And in what manere, 771
And hou he sat in grete destresse
Amonge þe pouere, & fenge almesse
Seuentene ȝere ; 774

LAUD 622

A-gayne xvij wyntersende,

COTTON

Whane he schowlde owte of þis worllde wend,

COTTON

Atte seuentene ȝeres ende,
he wuste he scholde heþen wende,
þorw grace of þe holi gost, 327
To Iesu crist, godus sone,
in blisse with him forte wone,
in lyf þat euer schal last. 330

VERNON

At þe seuenteþe ȝeres ende,
he wiste he scholde hennes wende,
þoru grace of þe holy gast, 327
To Iesu crist, godes sone,
In blisse of heuene ay forto wone,
In þe lif þat euere schal last. 330

LAUD 108

// þe while he was in þe house,
eche day he sey his spouse,
his fader & his moder. 345
Ac sone he tornede to þe wowe,
þat he nere not͛ y-knowe
of hem ne of non oþer. 348
// þis holy man þought͛ þo
þat his lif was almest͛ do
ffor seknesse þat he hadde. 351

LAUD 463

þe whyle he wonede in þe house,
Eche day he seȝ his spouse,
His fader & his moder. 345
Ac sone he wente him to þe wowe,
þat he neuere nere y-knowe
Of hem ne of non oþer. 348
¶ þe holy man him þoȝte þo
þat his lyf was almest ydo,
ffor siknesse þat he hadde. 351

TRINITY

And hou his frendes come*n* hym
    by,
And he hem knew ape*r*tely,
þat souȝtte*n* hym fer & nere ; 777
And hou he stale a-way he*m* fro,
þat non hym knew of alle þo,
So chaunged was his chere ; 780

(66)

¶ And hou þe ymage of oure lefdy
þe sergeauntz hete apertely,
In, hym, forto take, 783
And byd his bedes in þe chirche,
Goddes werkes þere to wirche,
His sorouȝ forto slake ; 786
And hou þat folk com fer & wyde
To þat chirche in vche syde,
hono*u*r hym forto make ; 789

LAUD 622

And hou he stale away he*m* fro,
And wolde nouȝth be honoured so,
bot libbe in woo & wrake ; 792

(67)

¶ And hou he wolde to tars haue
    went,
And whiche a tempest god hym sent,
þat droof hem to Romeyne ; 795
And hou he bad his fader good
herberewe & oþer lyues food,
He wroot forsoþe to seyne ; 798
And hou he seiȝ seuentene ȝere
ffader, & moder, & wijf þere,
wiþ sorouȝ & mychel peyne ; 801
And he wolde hem nouȝth yknowe,
Bot bare hym boþe symple & lowe,
þat had ben Man of meyne. 804

LAUD 622

---

he prayd hym þat brout hys mete,
Prev[i]ly he shoulde hym gete

COTTON

A lytyll ynke and perchemyne, 265
And all hys lyffe he wrote there In.

COTTON

He gat hi*m* enke & p*ar*chemyn ;
al his lyf he wrot þer-in,
as he hedde i-lyued here, 333
And radde hit siþe*n* vchadel,
he þonked god, so mihte he wel,
wiþ ful bliþe chere. 336

VERNON

// he gat him enke & p*ar*chemyn ;
And al his lif he wrot þer-In,
þat he had lyued here, 333
And radde it seþen eueri-del,
& þonkede god, so myȝt he wel,
Wiþ ful bliþe chere. 336

LAUD 108

---

parchemyn he þer' wan,
& al his lif wrot þer-on
as he lay on bedde. 354
¶ Also he wrot on his bok,
hou he his ȝong wif forsok,
þo he of londe wolde ; 357
hou his mantel he hire betok,
And his girdel he forsok,
& his ring of golde. 360

LAUD 463

Parchemyn he him wan,
And al his lyf wrot þer-an,
As he lay in his bedde. 354
¶ Al he wrot opon his bok,
How he his ȝonge wyf forsok,
þo he of londe wolde. 357
How he his mantel here by-tok,
And his gerdel þat was so guod,
And a ryng of golde. 360

TRINITY

(68)

¶ Iesus, þat is kyngⁱ of glorie,
his martirdom & his victorie
Sei3, & his trauaile ;   807
And whan he had his lijfⁱ ywrite,
he hidde þere noman shulde ywite,
his bookⁱ of gode paraile.   810
Priuelich Alex it bare,
þat noman mi3th þerof be-ware
Hou mychel it wolde auaile ;   813

And, whan he dyed, I vnderstonde
It was founden in his ri3th honde,
writen wiþouten faile.   816

(69)

¶ On palme sonenday, after messe,
In þe chirche amonge þe presse,
A voice com, I 3ou rede,   819
ffrom heuene adoune, wel shille & clere,
þat seide to hem in þis manere,
where-of many gonne drede,   822

LAUD 622   LAUD 622

---

whan hit was wretyn, he hit Folde,
¹And In his hand he gan hit hollde.
And a none he dyed, I wys, [¹leaf 150]

And dyght his sowlle to hewyn
  blys.   270
That ylke a daye in tym of masse,

COTTON   COTTON

¶ Whon he hedde don as i ou say,
vppon þe holy son[e]day
þat com aftur nest,   339
With muche Ioie & muche li3t
his soule, þat was so feir & bri3t,
went out of his brest.   342

Whan he hadde I-do as I 3ou say,
Vpon þe holy soneday
þat com after nest,   339
Wiþ meche ioye & meche ly3th,
his soule, þat was so fair & bry3th,
Wente out at his brest.   342

Whon þat gost was went to heuene,
þer com a vois with milde steuene
in-to an holy stede,   345
þere as þe folk of Rome were,
godus seruise forte here,
& biddynge of holy bede,   348

When his soule was went to heuene,
þer com a vois wiþ milde stephene
In-to an holy stede,   345
þer al þe folk of rome were,
Godes seruise forto here,
To bidden holy bede,   348

VERNON   LAUD 108

// It befel on a sonenday
þat alle men of cristes lay
to þe chirche come ;   363
Clerkes, knyghtes, 3ongⁱ & olde,
þemperour, wiþ eorles bolde,
þe pope self of Rome,   366

¶ þat fel opon a soneday,
þat alle men of cristis lay
To þe cherche come,   363
Clerkes, kny3tes, 3onge & olde,
þe emperour with his erles bolde,
þe Pope self of Rome.   366

// þo þei þidere come were
to her', as þei sholde þere,
Godes seruise,   369
Alle þei beden here bede ;
Be þe liftⁱ þei herde grede,
In wonder wise :   372

¶ þo hy þuder y-come were,
To here al so hy sholde þere
Hare seruise.   369
Al so hy hare bedes bede,
In þe luft hy herde grede,
In a wonder wise :   372

LAUD 463   TRINITY

And seide, '3ee þat trauailed be
In hunger & þurst for loue of me,
Comeþ! I shal 3ou fede, 825
In heuene, þat is so fair & bri3th,
þare euere is day & neuere ni3th,
And ioye wiþouten drede.' 828
(70)
¶ þe poeple & þe clergie,
ffor þat voice songen þe letanye
wiþ gode deuocioun; 831
LAUD 622

And bisou3tten þe heuene kyng',
þat he shulde 3iue hem tokenyng'
ffro heuene to erþe adoun, 834
Of þe voice what it were
þat among' hem com þere
wiþ so mery soun. 837
þe voice com eft' anoþer tyme,
And seide as I schal seie in
Ryme;
Herkneþ þis resoun: 840
LAUD 622

---

whan all fowlke att chirche was,
A woyce cam frome þe trinite
To the bysshope of that cyte. 274
COTTON

'Com to me,' he sayde, 'þat woll
swynke, [drynke;
And I schall gywe yowe met and
COTTON

And seide þis word with-outen fayle:
'comeþ to me, þat haueþ trauayle
or tene for mi sake; 351
Comeþ to me, i schal ou fille
with ioy & blisse, & al or wille,
þat neuermore schal slake.' 354
Whon þei hedde þis wordus herd,
þei weren vchone sore a-ferd,
& fullen a-doun to grounde. 357
As þei le3e & hudde heor face,
þer com eft, þorw godus grace,
in a luytel stounde, 360
VERNON

And seyde þes wordes wiþoute faille:
"Comeþ to me, þat haueþ trauaille
Oþer charge for my sake! 351
Comeþ to me, I schal 3ou fille
Wiþ ioye & blisse at al 3oure wille,
þat neuere mor schal slake." 354
Whan þe folk hadde þat word herd,
þe[i] were echone sore a-fered
& fullen doun to grounde; 357
As þei leyen & hedde here face,
þar com owth, þoru godes grace,
In a litel stounde, 360
LAUD 108

¶ 'Comeþ alle now to me,
þat sinful haueþ .y.-beo,
And afong' 3oure meode. 375
Alle þat haueþ þolede pine,
ffor þe loue of me & myne,
I. 3ou wile feode.' 378
// Of þis steuene hem þoughte wonder,
Many wende it were thonder,
to gronde þei gonne falle. 381
what þis cry betokne sholde,
þat god hem shewe wolde
A kneo[1] þei beden alle. [¹ MS. keneo] 384
LAUD 463

¶ 'Comeþ alle now to me,
þat synful haueþ for me y-be,
And a-fongeþ 3oure mede. 375
Alle þat haueþ y-þoled pyne,
Honger and þerst for loue myne,
Ich 3ow wille fede.' 378
¶ Of þis steuene hem þo3te wonder;
ffele wende it were þonder;
To gronde hy gonne falle. 381
What þis cry be-tokny sholde,
þat god hem sone schewy wolde,
A-kneo hy beden alle. 384
TRINITY

(71)
¶ ' þere is a Man of dedes gode,
Spirituel, & mylde of mode,
Now in Rome Cite ;   843
In penaunce he is ȝou amonge,
Certeynly ȝee ne shullen nouȝth longe
here in erþe hym see ;   846
A gode fridayes morowenyng�
he shal wende to heuene kyngⁱ,
þat sytteþ in trinite.   849

LAUD 622

Takeþ wiþ hym þe riȝth pace
To þe chirche of seint Boneface
wiþ grete solempnite.'   852
(72)
¶ þai souȝtten hym & nouȝth ne founde,
And hadden many morouȝful stounde,
Til þe gode fryday ;   855
wiþ gret deuocioun amongⁱ,
Of bedes & of chirche songⁱ, [leaf 25, bk]
To god þai maden her pray ;   858

LAUD 622

'Sek ye vpe my serwaunte, where þat
   he be,   277
That he maye praye for this cete.'
oHde and yonge, lesse and more,

COTTON

AH hard this þat were there :   280
For hit was no man, lewde ne
   leryd,
But of this woyce he nas a-Feryd.

COTTON

Anoþer steuene milde & meke,
& bad þei schulde ris vp, & seke
A godus mon of Rome,   363
' þat ȝe mowe, þorwȝ his preȝere,
of his godnes ben partinere
atte day of dome.'   366
¶ þei risen Al vp with bliþe chere,
& souȝte boþe fer and nere,
bi wei and [eke] bi strete.   369
And for noþing þat þei wrouȝte,
with þat relik þat þei souȝte
mouȝte þei nowhere mete,   372

VERNON

Anoþer stephene mylde & meke,
& bad hem vp arise, & seke
A godes man of rome,   363
' þat ȝe mowe, þoru his preyer,
Of his godnesse ben partener
At þe day of dome.'   366
// þei risen alle wiþ bliþe chere
& southe boþe fer & nere,
Be weye & ek be strete ;   369
Bote for noþing þat þei wrouth,
Wiþ þat relyk þat þei south,
Myȝtte þe[i] nowar mete ;   372

LAUD 108

// Alle þat þer-inne were
Herde ȝet¹ an noþer bere,
Riȝht about¹ noñ.   387
' Goþ, besecheþ godes knyght,
þat crist¹ serueþ day & nyght¹,
þat he bidde for Rome.'   390
¶ þe pope & his clerkes alle [lf 117, bk]
Adoun on kneo þei gon falle,
Beforne & behynde,   393

LAUD 463

¶ Alle þat þer-ynne were,
I-herde ȝut anoþer bere,
Riȝt aboute none :   387
' Goþ, by-sechest godis knyȝt,
þat crist serueþ day and nyȝt,
þat he bidde for Rome.'   390
þe Pope and his clerkes alle
A-doun on kneo gonne falle,
By-fore & ek¹ be-hynde,   393

TRINITY

þai praiden hym for his pyte,
And for his mychel humilite,
þat he hem sent' to say 861
where was þe Man þe Aungel of tolde
Twyes er þan wiþ wordes bolde,
þat in swiche payne lay. 864
(73)
¶ þe þridł tyme com þe voice
ffro hym þat was don on croice

LAUD 622

wiþ gret solempne liȝth, 867
And seide, 'wendeþ wiþoute soioure
To Eufeniens þe Cenatoure,
ffor þere he lijþ vche niȝth. 870
Swiþe good haþ ben his lijf';
His werkes shullen be made rijf';
His soule is fair & briȝth.' 873
þat ilk' tyme, as I ȝou seie,
His gost went' þe riȝth weie
ffro þe body to god almiȝth. 876

LAUD 622

Goddes seruaunte anon was sought,
but who hit was þey knowe hym nought; 284
That voyce sayde on that ylke a daye,

COTTON

And tolde hym redyly where he laye;
'In eufamyans hous,' he sayde, 'is he, 287
That hathe my Serwaunt long I-be.'

COTTON

Til þat vois, with wordes meke,
com a-ȝein & bad hem seke
in Eufemians house; 375
ffor þere scholde þei sone fynde
þat scholde hele doumbe & blynde,
a relik preciouse. 378
¶ þen þei ede sone anan,
& asked sire Eufemian
ȝif he kneuȝ such a mon. 381
He onswerde ful rediliche,
'i sigge ou lordingus sikerliche
of such ne wot i non.' 384

VERNON

Til þat voitȝ wiþ worde meke
Com aȝen, & bad hem seke
In sire Eufemianes hous, 375
'þer ȝe scholle sone fynde
þat schal hele dombe & blynde,
A relik precious.' 378
þanne wente þei forþ a-nan,
& askeden sire eufemian:
ȝif he knew swich a man. 381
he ansuerede redely
& seyde: lordingges, sikerly,
Of swich ne wot I non. 384

LAUD 108

And bede god Almyghty king'
// þat he hem sende som tokenyng'
wher' þei myghte him fynd. 396
Iesu Crist', þat is so mylde,
Reuthe hadde of þis childe,
þat is in care bounde. 399
To hem seide heuene spouse,
'Goþ to Eufemianes house,
þer' he worþ y.-founde.' 402

LAUD 463

¶ And bede god almyȝty kyng',
þat hem sende som toknyng'
Wher þorgh hy myȝte him fynde. 396
Iesu crist, þat is so mylde, [leaf 76]
Ruthe hadde of þis childe,
þat was in care y-bounde. 399
To hem he seyde, þe heuene spouse,
'Goþ to Eufemia[ne]s house,
þere he worþ y-founde.' 402

TRINITY

(74)

¶ þe holy pope Innocent
And þe Emperoures swiþe went,
Sire Eufeniens to calle,　　　879
And chalenged hym in þis manere,
Eufeniens & his wijft yfere,
Riȝth amonge hem alle ;　　　882
'In þine house is, þat is so meke,
Goddes man þat we seke ;
Hou may þis cas bifalle ?　　　885
we haue ysouȝth hym fer & wyde,
Hou darstou goddes sergeaunt hyde
In boure oiþer in halle ?'　　　888

(75)

¶ Eufeniens ansuered sone,
As he auȝtte forto done,
To þe pope Innocent,　　　891

LAUD 622

And seide, þeiȝ he shulde deye,
Of swiche a Man couþe he nouȝth seye,
By god omnipotent,[1] ;　　　[1 MS. omnipototent]
'ffor swiche a Man ȝif I knewe,
ffayn I wolde hym to ȝou shewe
Treuly wiþ god entent.'　　　897
þan seiden þe Cardinales twelue,
'God ȝeue þat it were þi-selue
Byfore vs in present.'　　　900

(76)

¶ In þat tyme tweie emperoures
Of Rome kepten þe honoures
wiþ her cristen menee ;　　　903
þat on hete Archadius,
And þat oþere Honorius ;
þai weren hende & fre.　　　906

LAUD 622

---

the besshope And þe emperour　289
went in to euffamyans hous ;
They axyd hym of syche a man ;

COTTON

he sayde he knwe there of noone.
on of his seruaunttes was thane thore,　　　293

COTTON

¶ þenne wente forþ þe Emperours,
Archadius & honorius,
& Inocent þe Pope,[1]　　　[1 Pope eras't]
Anon to Eufemians in,—
er þei weore þer, wolde þei not blin,—
with hem a god gret frape.　　　390
þen com a knaue sone a-nan,
& seide to sire Eufemian,
'go we, sire, i rede,　　　393

VERNON

þanne wente forþ þe emperuors,
Archadious & honorius,
& Inocent þe pape,　　　387
Anon to sire Eufemia[n]s In ;
Til þei come þere, wolde þei nat blyn ;
Wiþ hem wente forþ greth frape.　390
þanne cam forþ a knaue anan,
& seyde to sire eufemian :
'Go we, sire, I rede,　　　393

LAUD 108

// After þis steueñ vp þei stod,
& heried god wiþ glad moed,
Alle þat þere were.　　　405
ffor nought þe pope was so gram,
Eufemian he vndernam
wiþ wel sterne bere :　　　408

LAUD 463

¶ After þis steuene, op hy stode,
And herede god with glade mode,
Alle þat þer were.　　　405
ffor noȝt þe Pope was ful gram,
Eufemian he vnder-nam,
With wel sterne bere :　　　408

TRINITY

wiþ Eufeniens þai wenten riȝth
fforto fecchen goddes kniȝth,
þat was so good of fe.   909
Ac eufeniens was swiþe liȝth,
And went bifore his hous to diȝth
wiþ gretˀ solempnite   912
(77)
¶ Eufeniens, whan he hom cam,
Al his meignee he vndernam,
ȝif þat þai euere ysowe   915
Any Man þat so holy were
As þe Aungel tolde of ere,
Of his meignee to knowe.   918
Alexius wardeyn com þan,
And seide, 'sir, it is ȝoure bede-
   man,
þat liþ ded by þe wowe;   921
      LAUD 622

He þat þou hast so longe yfedˀ,
wiþ mete & drynkˀ, clooþ &. bedˀ,
He bare hym euer lowe.   924
(78)
¶ 'I trowe wel it may so be,
whom so ȝee seche, þat it is he,
ffor he was good of lijfˀ;   927
His bedes he bad as a frere,
Ne wolde he nouȝth, while he was
   here,
Louen fiȝth ne strijfˀ;   930
A bookˀ in his honde he haltˀ
Swiþe fast, & narewe yfaltˀ,
who þat it couþe descryue;   933
I ne wootˀ what he þereinne wrouȝth;
þe parchemyn I hym bouȝth,
Gon fourty dayes & fyue.'   936
      LAUD 622

That stode and lokeyd Alex by-
   fore.
'Syr,' he sayde, 'I trowe hit be
      COTTON

[1] That poreman þat yee toke to me,
That long has bene in your haƚƚ, 297
he is an holy man with aƚƚ.' [1 lf 150, bk]
      COTTON

And loke, sire, at oure pilgrime,
þat ȝe han fed in long tyme,
wher he beo quik or dede.   396
'ȝif he be ded þat was so meke,
he is þat mon þat þei seke,
i wot, with-outen drede.   399
He was a mon of holy lif,
of him com neiþer cheste ne strif,
ne vuel word ne dede.'   402
      VERNON

And loken [sire] at ȝoure pilgrim
þat ȝe han fed of long tym,
Wher he be quik oþer dede.   396
'ȝif he be ded þat was so meke,
he is þat man þat þei seke,
I wot wiþ-oute drede :   399
he was a man of holy lif,
Of him com neuere stout ne strif,
Ne wikke word ne dede.'   402
      LAUD 108

¶ 'wikke man, whi hastou hydˀ,
þat he ne moste er beo kydˀ,
þe holy man!'   411
þe emperour began to chide,
& fele oþerˀ þat stode beside
towardˀ Eufemian.   414
      LAUD 463

'O luþer man, why hastow y-hud
þat he ne moste er be y-kud,
þulke holy man?'   411
¶ þe emperour be-gan to chyde,
And fele þat þer stode be-syde,
To-ward Eufemian.   414
      TRINITY

(79)

¶ þoo þat þis herden þe Emperoures
And oþere lordes of honoures,
þai þankeden god almiȝth. 939
He led hem þere lay þat body,
Clene & fair, & sumdel rody,
fface feir & briȝth. 942

LAUD 622

þe on Emperoure his honde vp took,
And wolde haue taken out þe book
þat was fair of siȝth; 945
Alexius þe book helde þoo;
þan was þe Emperour swiþe woo,
And in his herte afliȝth. 948

LAUD 622

This ryche man went to hym a noone,
And founde Alex ded as ony stone,
But his vysage was allso bryght 301
As the sonne on þe daye lyght.
Than trowyd well eufemyan
That he was an holey man ; [rowres
he callyd þe bysshopes & þe Empe-

COTTON

To se þat cors so presyowse. 306
In theye com a non ryght,
And saue the body þat was so bryght;
downe on knes theye fell thow, 309
And oþer many that were þere moo,
And thankyd god In trinite,
That theye myght his seruaunte see.

COTTON

Whon Eufemian hedde þis herd,
he ron to loke hou Alix ferd,
in-to his hous ful riȝt. 405
He fond him ded whon he com pare,
his visage þer hit lay al bare,
as sonne hit schined briȝt. 408
In his hond he heold a skrit,
Eufemian sturte him forþ as tit,
to wite what was þer-Inne. 411
Bote with non scunes ginne
of þe hond þat hit was Inne
miȝte he hit not out winne. 414

VERNON

Whanne eufemian þat i-herde,
he ȝede to loke hou alex ferde,
To his hous ful ryȝth ; 405
[1]he fond him ded whan he com þare,
his face, þer it lay on bere, [1 leaf 236]
As sonne schinede bryȝth. 408
In his hond he fond a skript,
Eufemian ȝede to him as tyd
To wyte what was þer-Inne ; 411
Bote for nones kynnes gyn
out of þe hond þat it was In
Myȝtte he it nat wynne. 414

LAUD 108

// Naþeles wiþ hem he ȝeode,
þe pope & many of þe theode,
toward his hous þo. 417
þe pope self & þemperour
Sought halle, þei souhte bour,
so wel so þei coude go ; 420
// þei soughte him one stounde,
atte laste þei him founde,
þer' he lay on bedde. 423
thoruh an hyne hem tolde be mouþe,
þat of his lyf mychel couþe,
And hem y-wissed hedde. 426

LAUD 463

¶ Naþeles, with him hy ȝede,
þe Pope, and manye of hare dede
To-ward þis house. 417
þe Pope self and þe emperour,
Hy soȝte halle, hy soȝte bour,
So wel so hy couþe. 420
¶ Hy soȝte him one stounde,
Ac atte laste hy him founde,
þer he lay in his bedde, 423
þorgh an hyne of the house,
þat moche of his lyf couþe,
þat hem y-wissed hedde. 426

TRINITY

(80)

¶ þe Emperour þoo speke bigan,
And seide vnto þe body þan,
þere it lay in þe herne ;
'þou3 we ben Men of synful lijf,
Emperours we ben wiþouten strijf,
Rome forto gouerne ; 954

we defenden holy chirche
A3eins hem þat wolden wirche
Dedes stoute & sterne ; 957
þerfore delyuer vs þi book,
þat þe poeple þere-on mowe look,
wisdom forto lerne.' 960

LAUD 622   LAUD 622

The bysshope, as he stode hym nye,
A perchement leffe in his honde he
  see, 314
But he hyllde his hand so faste,
That owte he myght hit natt wrast.
'Sonne,' sayde þe bysshope, 'I praye
  þee 317

that in thye honde þoue lett me see ;
Synfulle all thou3e hit bee,
I haue powre and dyngnytee 320
For to lousse and for to bynde
Thym þat I in syn Fynde. [leaf 151]
There Fore, sone, let me wetten
what ys in thy bocke wrytyn.' 324

COTTON   COTTON

¶ Whon he mihte no betere spede,
to þe Emperour he ede,
and tolde þat tiþande. 417
þenne come þei boþe forþ god pas,
til þei come þer hit was,
þe dede cors liggande. 420
whon þei come in-to þe hous,
þis Emperours þei seiden þus,
and on þis Maneere : 423
'þau3 we for sunne are vnworþi,
we han kepinge not forþi
of þeos londes heere. 426

Whan he ne my3tte no betere spede,
To þe emperour he 3ede,
& tolde him þat tydingge. 417
þane comeþ he a3en god pas,
Til he comen þar he was,
þe dede corps liggynde. 420
Whan þei comen Into þe hous,
þe emperour seyde þus
And on þis manere : 423
"þei we for synne ben vn-worþi,
We han to kepyng nawth for-þi
of þese londes here ; 426

VERNON   LAUD 108

¶ Beforen þe bed þei stoden þo,
þe pope & þemperour also ;
ac þei ne dorste ouer him trine, 429
þei wende he wer' liues man ;
Ac his gost was out-gan,
Brought he was of pyne. 432
// Eufemian adoun bey3,
his hond his neb he vnwrey
wiþ michel drede. 435
So suete smel of him tey3,
þat alle þat wer' ney3,
wonder of him heuede. 438

¶ By-fore þe bed hy stode þo,
þe Pope and þe emperour al-so,
Ac hy ne dorste hem tryne. 429
Hy wende he were a lyues man,
Ac his gost was out a-gon,
I-bro3t he was of pyne. 432
Eufemian a-doun bei3,
His neb, his hondes, he vn-wrei3,
With wel mochel drede. 435
So swote breþ out of him tei3,
þat alle þat wer' þer nei3,
þer-of wonder hauede. 438

LAUD 463   TRINITY

(81)

¶ whan þai hadden so yseide,
Alexius, þere he was yleide,
Opened vp his honde; 963
To þe pope wolde he nouȝth forsake,
Bot lete hym þoo þe book᷎ vptake,
To rede þat he fonde. 966
þoo þapostoile had his book᷎, [leaf 26]
His chaunceler he it bitook᷎
To rede, I vnderstonde; 969
Othoo was his name,
A Man yholde of gode fame
Ouer al Rome londe. 972

LAUD 622

(82)

¶ þe book᷎ he red wiþ gode wille,
þe folk᷎ herkned & helde hem stille
wiþouten any boost᷎ 975
Til þe book᷎ was red & seide.
Alexius was bifore hem leide,
ffulfild᷎ of þe holy gost᷎. 978
þe chaunceler wel loude grad᷎
whan he þe book᷎ of Alexius rad᷎
Among᷎ þe cristen ost᷎; 981
hou he fro frendes gan wende,
And hou his fader fer & hende
Souȝth hym by euery cost; 984

LAUD 622

The beshope toke þe boke so hynde, That Alex hys hond on bynde;

COTTON   COTTON

'And þis Mon þat we pope[1] calle,
haþ þe pouwer of vs alle, [1 pope eras't]
and of al holichirche; 429
fforþi diliuere vp þat scrite,
þat we þer-þorwh mai seo and wite
hou we schul with þe worche.' 432

VERNON

"And þis man þat we pope calle,
haþ þe kepyng of vs alle
& of holy churche; 429
þerfore deliure vs vp þe skryt᷎,
þat we þere-þoru may se & wyt
hou we schulle wiþ þe werche." 432

LAUD 108

¶ Out of his mouþ þer stoed᷎ a leom̄
Brighter᷎ þan þe sonne beom̄,
þat al þe stede atende. 441
Adoun þei fellen al on kneo,
to thanke god᷎ þat is so freo
Of wonder þat he sende. 444
Toward᷎ god he gan his hondes holde,
A writ betwene þei seye folde,
þei þat wer᷎ þer-inne. 447
Eufemian adoun beyȝ,
þat writ᷎ he drow & ȝerne tey
he ne myght᷎ it out-winne. 450

LAUD 463

¶ Out of his mouth stod a lem
Briȝter᷎ þan þe sonne-bem,
þat al þe stede atende. 441
A-doun hy felle, alle on kneo,
To þonky god þat is so freo
Of wonder þat hem sende. 444
¶ Op to-ward god held his honde;
A writ be-twixe hy seȝe y-folde,
Hy þat wer᷎ þer-ynne. 447
Eufemian a-doun heiȝ,
þat writ he drouȝ & ȝerne teiȝ,
Ne myȝte he it wynne. 450

TRINITY

(83)

¶ And hou he was to þe Emperoure
ysent, to be Man of valoure
And lernen chiualrie, 987
Of huntyng⹀, & of Ryuere,
Of chesse pleieyng⹀ & of tablere :
Al nas worþ a flye ; 990
Leuer hym was to conne good,
And seruen god wiþ mylde mood,
and his moder Marie : 993
And hou he ȝede seuentene ȝer
In pilerinage fer & ner
wiþ mychel maladye ; 996

LAUD 622

(84)

¶ And oþer ȝeres seuentene
wiþ his fader he had ybene,
his bedeman by þe wowe, 999
þat fader ne moder ne his wijf
wisten of his holy lijf,
Ne þat he was hire owe ; 1002
And hou his fader sergeauntz alle,
veyn glorie gonne hym calle,
And gorre on hym gonne þrowe ; 1005
And hou he þe book ywriten hadde :
Of al his lijf, þere he it radde
To þe poeple heiȝe & lowe. 1008

LAUD 622

---

the beshope þat Rolle red A non,
That þey yt harde euerychone. 328

COTTON

There was there in redly tolde
Alle hys lyfe, yong and olde.

COTTON

¶ whon þei þus hedde iseid heor wille,
þe pope¹ leide his hond þer-tille,
& he þenne let hit go. [¹ pope eras't] 435
Anon þe pope¹ let rede hit þere,
bi-foren alle þat þer were,
heringe his fader Also. 438

VERNON

Wen þei hadde þus seid here wille,
þe pope leyde his hond þer-tille,
Alex þan let go. 435
þe pope as tyd let rede it þere
Byfore al þo þat þer were,
herynde his fader also. 438

LAUD 108

// þe pope her-of was adred.
In his herte god he bad,
þat him grante sholde, 453
þat writ þat was in his hond,
þat þei myhte it vnderstond,
betokne what it wolde. 456

¶ þe pope to þe bed beyȝ,
þe writ of his hond he teyȝ,
Right wiþ-outen gynne. 459
þat writ he began to sprede,
& to foren þe folk to rede,
þat weren þer-inne. 462

LAUD 463

¶ þe Pope her-of was a-drad,
In his herte, god he bad,
þat him granty sholde 453
þat writ þat was in his honde,
þat he myȝte it vnderstonde,
Be-tokny what it wolde. 456

¶ þe Pope to þe dede beiȝ ;
þat writ out of his hond he teiȝ,
Al with-oute gynne. 459
þat writ anon he gan sprede,
And by-fore hem alle rede,
þat þo wer' þerynne. 462

TRINITY

(85)

¶ þoo Eufeniens þise wordes herd,
Of his son hou it ferde,
Gret was his sorouȝeyng; 1011
His face he¹ rent, & his her. [¹ MS. his]
Men sorouȝed for hym fer & ner,
He fel in swowenyng. 1014
LAUD 622

On his owen son þat was,
His cry was euere, 'allas! allas!
deþ! why nyltou me stynge? 1017
Allas! sorouȝ! what is þi red?
þou hast me brouȝth vnto my ded;
Myne herte wil to-sprynge. 1020
LAUD 622

Whan hys Fader harde of thys,
That he was hys sone I wys, 332
'lorde,' he sayde, 'howe maye þys bee?
ys thys my sone þat I here scee?
Sewentene yere wyt All,
I had fynde hym in myn halle; 336
COTTON

I myght nat wyt for none Asaye,
What he was, nyght nor daye.
"leffe sone," he sayde, "why ded þou soo?
Thowe saw I was For þe Full woo;
for þowe were not At my wylle, 341
COTTON

¶ whon his fader hedde herd hit red,
he was a-wondred & a-dred,
for serwe he was neiȝ ded; 441
As mon þat hedde þe deþes wounde,
he fel a-doun to þe grounde
as heui as þe led. 444
whon he hedde longe i-leyn,
& his stat was comen aȝein,
he made reuþful chere. 447
He tar his cloþus & drouȝ his her,
with delful cri & siking sor,
þat del hit was to here. 450
VERNON

Whan his fader herde it rede,
he was for-wondred & for-drede,
for sorwe he was ney ded; 441
As man þat hadde deþes wounde
He fel swingge doun to grounde,
Heuy so any led. 444
Wan he hadde longe I-leyn,
þan his stat bi-com a-gayn,
& made reuly chere; 447
he rof his brest, he drou his her
wiþ duelful cry & syking sor,
þat pite it was to here. 450
LAUD 108

¶ þo eufemian was y-war
þat his sone lay þar,
& so long had wiþ him beo, 465
he fel in swounyng on þe molde,
'Allas,' he seide, 'þat euer .I. sholde
so vnkynde beo.' 468
// Be a stounde he gan vp-stonde,
Tar his her & wrong his honde,
þat þe folk myghte rewe. 471
þei weopen & made reuly cry,
for him þei wer wel sory
þat þei him euere knewe. 474
LAUD 463

¶ þo sir Eufemian was y-war
þat his sone lay þar,
His armes he to-spradde, 465
He tar his her, he tar his cloþ,
And fel a-swoȝe opon þe cors,
So moche sorwe he hadde. 468
¶ By a stounde he gan op-stonde,
To-tar his her & wrang his honde,
þat alle folk miȝte rewe; 471
¹He wep and made reuful cry;
ffor him hy were wel sory, [¹ leaf 76, bk]
þat he him er ne knewe. 474
TRINITY

(86)

¶ 'Now I may no ioye haue;
No confort ne may me saue;
My blis is al forlorne! 1023
ffor my son þat liþ here ded,
In elde he shulde haue ben my red.
Allas! þat I was borne! 1026
LAUD 622

O son, whi woldestou suffren smert,
And dye wiþ me here in pouert,
A begger as þou worne? 1029
To þi comyng was al my speire,
To haue ymade of þee myne eire,
Of londe, Castel & corne.' 1032
LAUD 622

And ewer more þou helde þe styll;
Thyne own s)aruantes þat sholde be,
myche harme ded þey to þee; 344
Theye kest water on thyn hede, [lf151, bk]
And gafe þe þat was in the dyche leuyde,
COTTON

And euer þou bare þe meke and lawe,
For þat no man should þe there cnawe.
In heuyn ther fore þou hast mede:
Sonne, praye fore me, fore I haue nede."' 350
COTTON

Muche dcol hit is to telle,
houȝ he on þat bodi felle
of weopyng blon he nouht. 453
He seide, 'Allas! mi dere sone,
hou miȝtest þou þus longe wone
with me þat kneuȝ þe nouht? 456
Allas! nou hastou dwelled here
al þis seuentene ȝere
in myn owne Inne; 459
And þou hast boren þe so lowe,
þat þou woldest neuere ben a-knowe
þat þou wer of mi kinne. 462
VERNON

Meche doel it is to telle
hou he on þat body felle,
of weping blan he nouth. 453
[. . . . .
. . . . . no gap in the MS.]
'Allas nou hastou duelled here
Alle þese seuentene ȝere
In myn owene In, 459
& þou hast boren þe so lowe,
& noldest neuere ben o knowe
þat þou were of oure kyn. 462
LAUD 108

¶ 'Awey, lord, þat herest my bone,
whi helestou my leoue sone
So long in my house, 477
þat wee ne moste him knowe,
And forȝete mychel wowe,
boþe .I. & my spouse. 480
// 'Awey, my sone, listou her,
& euer .I. hoped of þe to here
A-lyue þat þou were. 483
Me þenkeþ myn herte wile breke,
þat I. ne may wiþ þe speke.
Allas, þat .I. ded nere.' 486
LAUD 463

¶ "A-wey, lord, þat art vs a-boue,
Why hele þou my leue sone?
To longe in myn house, 477
þat we ne moste him y-knowe,
And for-ȝute oure wowe,
And kesse him with mouþe. 480
¶ A-wey, my sone, now listow here,
And euere ich hopede of þe y-here,
A-lyue þat þou were. 483
Me þenkeþ my herte wil breke,
Now þou ne miȝt with me speke,
A-wey þat ded y-nere." 486
TRINITY

(87)

¶ His moder herd þat tydynge;
ffor hir son she gan flynge
In Rage as a lyonesse;   1035
Sorouȝ-fullich her pleynt she made;
Noman miȝth hire herte glade,
Of al þe grete presse.   1038

LAUD 622

His fader had ylore þe speche;
To his moder was no leche
þat miȝth her cry acesse.   1041
Letted she nouȝth for al þe þrong,
þat she ne ran þe poeple among,
Hire son to clyppe & kysse.   1044

LAUD 622

---

hys moder lyued in In longyng,
whan sche herde of thys tydyng,
She com Forthe with A raply rese,
As A lyon lept oute of A lees;   354

COTTON

She weppyd And cryde sore,
As thay don þat arne woo.
'let me,' she sayd, ' my sone see;
I Fed hym on myn owne kee.'   358

COTTON

Allas! allas! and weilawai,
þat euere I a-bod þis day,
þis serwe forte seo.   465
I wende haue had of þe solas
in myn elde; Allas! Allas!
for deol ded wol i beo.'   468
¶ whon his Moder herde of þis,
heo sturte forþ in haste i-wis,
As A lyonesse;   471
with hirself heo ferde to wonder,
heo ter hir cloþus al in sunder,
in a gret woodnesse.   474

VERNON

Out ay, allas, & weylawey,
þat I euere a-bod þis day
þis sorwe forto se!   465
I wende han had of þe solas
In myn elde, allas, allas,
for doel ded willi be!'   468
Whenne his moder herde of þis,
ȝe sterte forþ in haste i-wis
as a leonesse,   471
Wiþ hire sulf sche ferde to wonder,
Sche rof hire cloþes al to sonder
In a gret wodnesse;   474

LAUD 108

¶ þe noyse into þe bour sprong
of þe sorwe was hem among,
þat in þe halle were.   489
his moder was wel sory,
& axed what were þat cry
þat she herde wiþ ere.   492
// Of hir sone men tolde anon,
þat out while was y.-gon,
& hou he was y.-founde,   495
& hou he hadde þer-inne woned,
& þis werldes blisse shoned,
And tholed harde stounde.   498

LAUD 463

¶ þe drem in-to þe bour sprong,
Of sorwe þat hem was among,
þat in þe halle were.   489
His moder lay þere wel sory,
And axste what were al þat cry
þat hy herde with ere.   492
¶ Of here sone me tolde anon,
þat out whyle was a-gon,
And how he was y-founde;   495
And how he hadde þer-ynne y-woned,
And al þis worldis blesse y-shoned,
And þolede wel harde stounde.   498

TRINITY

(88)

¶ "O son, þat soke of myne pappes,
þou hast' ysent' me sory happes,
þus sone art' went' me fro.　　1047
I wende haue yhad of þee solas;
Myne hope is tynt, allas! allas!
And welþe is went' to woo.　　1050
　　　LAUD 622

Son, þou doest vs stronge tourment'!
Oure ioye is al away went'!
ffor sorouȝ we shullen vs sle;　　1053
ffor often þou seiȝ þi fader & me
Erlich & late wepe for þee,
And ek' þi wijf also.　　1056
　　　LAUD 622

---

whan she hym sawe, she Fylle downe,
All was A waye here Resonne.
whan she rose she stoode hym by,
She kyssyde hym, And sayd on hye,
　　　COTTON

'Sonne,' she sayde, And wept Full
　　sore,　　363
'Nowe schall I speke with þe no
　　more.
　　　COTTON

Heo drouȝ hir her as heo weore wod,
& seide, 'for him þat died on rod,
Men, ȝe ȝiue me way,　　477
þat I mai to mi sone go;
was neuer Moder half so wo
as me is þis day.　　480
ȝif me roum, & let me se
þe bodi þat was boren of me,
and fed of my breste.　　483
Let me come þat cors to,
for wel ȝe witen hit is skil so
þat i beo hit nexte.'　　486
　　　VERNON

Sche drou hire her as sche were wod,
& seyde: "for him þat deyde on rod,
ȝe men, ȝiueþ me wey,　　477
þat I may to my sone go!
Was neuere moder half so wo
As me is þis day.　　480
ȝiueþ me roum, & lat me se
þe body þat was boren of me,
& fed was of my brest!　　483
leteþ me come þe cors vntil,
ffor ȝe wyten þat it is skyl
þat I be it next."　　486
　　　LAUD 108

¶ þo she herde of hir' sone,
þat he was aȝein come,
out of bedde she sprong';　　501
Al hir' ȝuel she forȝat',
And hardiliche held hir' gate
Al þat folk' among'.　　504
// 'war anon, par charite,
Let' me go my sone to seo,
And myn oune fode.'　　507
þe teres felle to hir' kneo,
þat al þe folk' myhte seo
þe brest' orn al o blode.　　510
　　　LAUD 463

¶ þo hy herde of here sone,
How he was aȝen y-come,
Of here bedde hy sprong';　　501
Al hyre euel hy for-ȝat,
And hardeliche a-doun stap,
þe folk' alle among':　　504
¶ 'Remeþ me, for godis lone,
And leteþ me go to my sone,
I se myn owene fode.'　　507
þe teres felle to here kneo,
þat al þat folk' myȝte wel y-seo,
Hire brest al a-blode.　　510
　　　TRINITY

(89)	ffilþe & foule vryne, 1059
¶ 'þo þat þee shulden haue serued trewe,	And beten þee ofte swiþe sore;
ffele tymes on þee þai þrewe	And þou suffredest euermore,
	And took' it nouȝth to pyne. 1062
LAUD 622	LAUD 622

Thowe hast be sought in meny A londe,	With messengerys, And with sonde,
COTTON	COTTON

Whon heo miȝte neiȝe hit neer,	Whan sche myȝtte neyh it nere,
heo fel þer-on with deolful cher,	Sche fel þer-on wiþ sori chere,
& seide, 'Allas! mi sone, 489	& seyde: "allas, my son, 489
Whi woldestou þus with us fare,	Whi hauest tou þus wiþ vs fare,
to leten vs dwellen in serwe & care?	Suffred vs for þe sorwe & care,
whi hastou þus done? 492	Whi hastou þus don? 492
þou hast i-seȝen þi fader and me	þou hast i-seye þi fader & me
wepen & maken gret del for þe,	Wepen & maken gret doel for þe
boþe erly and late; 495	Boþe erly & late; 495
And þou hast seuentene ȝer	And tou hast seuentene ȝer
vnknowen i-dwelled mid vs her,	Vn-knowe duelled wiþ vs her
in pore beggers state.' 498	In pouere beggeres state." 498
Ofte-siþes heo fel doun	Ofte-siþe ȝe fel doun
on þat dede cors al in swoun,	opon þe body al I-swoun,
and custe hondes and feet; 501	& kissede honden & feet; 501
And þat face þat was so swete,	& þat face þat was so swete,
heo custe hit & mad hit wete	Sche it kiste, & made it wete
with teres þat heo leet. 504	Wiþ teres þat sche let. 504
VERNON	LAUD 108

¶ So sone so she to him come, [lf 118]	¶ So sone þo hy to him com,
vpon þe liche she fel y.-lome,	Ope þe lich hy fel anon,
And kiste it wel ȝerne. 513	And keste it wel ȝerne; 513
she kist' his neb, she kiste his hond',	Hy keste his neb and his honde,
on þe liche she lay, & nolde not wond',	Ope þe lich hy lay wel longe,
Mighte noman hire werne. 516	Hire ne myȝte noman werne; 516
// 'Allas, my sone, my dere lyf,	¶ "A-wey, my sone, þou were my lyf!
Soriere nas neuere wif	Sorwere nas y-neuere wyf,
þan .I. am for þe nouþe. 519	þan ich am for þe nouþe. 519
ffor .I. hopede euer' þe to seo,	ffor euere ich hopede þe to seo,
Er .I. diede, & speke wiþ þe,	Er ich deye, and speke with þeo,
And kisse þe wiþ mouþe. 522	And kesse þe with mouþe. 522
LAUD 463	TRINITY

why woldestou cast þee in care,	Of alle þise seuentene ȝere
Of hem to suffre swiche bysmare,	Ne woldestou noman tellen here
þat weren þine owen hyne? 1065	þou come of body myne." 1068

LAUD 622   LAUD 622

Bot there was no man myght þe see,   lewe sonne, þou praye for mee, [leaf 152]
And euer þou sat be owre knee. 368   That I may þe in bleyss see.'

COTTON   COTTON

Heo seide, 'allas! þat me is wo,	Sche seide: "allas, what me is wo!
þou were my sone with-outen mo,	¹þou were my sone wiþ-oute mo;
wepeþ alle wiþ me. 507	Wepeþ al folk wiþ me! [¹ leaf 236, back]
Ichaue þe fed moni a day,	I haue þe fed many a day;
Allas! sone, weilaway,	Allas owt & weylawey,
þat i ne knewh not þe. 510	þat I ne knew nout þe! 510
þou mist haue be a gret lordyng,	þou myȝtest han ben a greth lording,
and ben honoured as a king,	& honured als a kyng,
ȝif hit hedde beo þi wille. 513	ȝif it hadde ben þi wille; 513
Nou hastou had despit and wrong	Nou hauest þou had despit & wrong
of þi þralles euer among,	Of þine þralles euere among,
and boren hit ful stille. 516	& bor[e]n it ful stille. 516
Allas! ho schal ȝiue to me	Allas, who schal ȝiue to me
welle of teres to wepe for þe	Welle of teres to wepe for þe
boþe dai and niht? [leaf 44, back] 519	Boþe day & nyȝth? 519
Allas! allas! me is wo,	Allas allas, what me is wo!
icholde myn herte wolde breken a-two,	I wolde myn herte it breke a-tuo
þat i saiȝ nou þis siht.' 522	þat I ne saye nowth þis syȝth." 522

VERNON   LAUD 108

¶ Ac Al myn hope is y.-lore,	¶ Ac al myn hope is y-lore,
Nou þou list ded me before,	Now þou list ded me by-fore,
& wiþ me ne myght speke. 525	And with me ne myȝt speke. 525
Lord Crist, .I. bidde þin ore,	'Lord crist, ich bidde þyn ore,
Ne let me liuen namore,	Ne let þou me lyue namore,
ac let myn herte breke.' 528	Ac let myn herte breke.'" 528
// She wrong hir hondes & siked sore,	¶ Hy wrang here hond, and siȝte sore,
And to tar hire lokkes hore,	To-tar here shroud, here lokkes hore,
As she were woed. 531	As hy were wod. 531
'Leoue sone, bidde .I. þe,	'Leue sone, by-seche ich þe,
Let me dien nou wiþ þe,	þou lete me deye now byfore þe,
Mi lyf nis not goed.' 534	þe lyf me nis noȝt guod.' 534

LAUD 463   TRINITY

(90)

¶ fforþ com þoo his trewe wijf,
wiþ sorouȝ, & care & drery lijf,
And neiȝ for doel dedł.   1071
'Allas! she seide, my ioye cast,
Kare & sorouȝ ben in me fast,
As widewe wiþoute redł.   1074
   LAUD 622

Al my welþe is fro me went,
No womman is in swiche tourment
In lengþe ne in brede. [leaf 26, bk] 1077
Al þis werlde, & it myne were,
I wolde ȝiue it fer and nere,
To seen his fairehede.   1080
   LAUL 622

hys wyfe þat was In chamber stokyn,
Of þys tydynges harde sche spokyn;
She com forthe in A sempyll pace,
Sory, I wott, welle þat che was;   374
She swonnyd at þe fryst syght,
   COTTON

That on here was blake, þat rest was wyght.
Than she sayd with mylde chere,
'Where hastowe be, my leman dere?
Full long I myght þe A-byde,
   COTTON

¶ þenne com forþ a dreri þing,
i-cloþed in cloþus of mournyng,
þat was his owne wyue.   525
Heo wepte þat pite was to se,
and seide, 'Allas! þat wo is me,
þat euere hedde I lyue.   528
Nou al my ioye a-wei is gon,
er hedde i hope, nou habbe i non
to seon him a-lyue.   531
Nou am i widewe, allas! þe stounde,
serwe haþ ȝiue myn herte a wounde,
þat me to deþ wol driue.   534
   VERNON

// þanne cam forþ a drery þing,
I-clad in cloþes of mournyng,
It was Alex wif;   525
Sche wep þat pite was to se
& seyde: "Allas, ful wo is me,
þat euere hadde I lyf!   528
Nou al my ioye awey is gon.
Er hadde I hope, now haue I non
To sen him on lyue;   531
Nou am I wydewe, allas þat stounde!
Sorwe haþ ȝiuen myn herte a wounde
þat me to deþe schal dryue.   534
   LAUD 108

¶ Sone þo com his wif,
þat louede him as hir lyf,
To þe hous ago.   537
So sone so she com him to,
betwene hire armes she gan him fo,
& kissed his mouþe þo.   540
// 'Awey, my leof, what hastou do?
whi hastou holde þe so
In þin oune house,   543
þat non ne most com þe to,
So freond auȝte to oþer do,
Ne .I. þat was þi spouse?   546
   LAUD 463

¶ Sone þer-after com his wyf,
þat louede him more þan here lyf,
In-to þulke house.   537
So sone so hy com him to,
Be-twixe here armes hy gan him fo,
And keste him with mouþe;   540
¶ "A-wey! my lef, what hastow y-do?
Why hastow þe y-heled so,
In þyn owene house,   543
þat þou ne woldest come me to,
So frend oȝte to oþer do,
Ne ich þat was þy spouse?   546
   TRINITY

(91)

¶ 'It is no wonder of my doloure;
Yshadewed is al my myroure[1],
And lorne is my briȝthnesse; 1083
Myne herte may nouȝth lange dure.
Cursed worþe þou, dame auenture,
þat doost me destresse! [1 MS. myrouþe]

LAUD 622

After fair weder falleþ reyn,
After wynnyng' wep ageyn,
And care is after kysse, 1089
Erly to day by þe morowe,
I ne wist of care ne of sorowe :
To bale is tourned my blisse.' 1092

LAUD 622

Fore thowe hast soughte pylgermages
 wyde. 380
Thowe hast beene frome long,
Forsothe I haue done þe no wrong;
Wyghe þe speke nowe I ne maye,
Nowe maye I weddowe be for Aye,

COTTON

I maye be weddow And mayden dde,
And I haue done as ye me bade.
Thowe weddest me to be þy Free,
O nyght togeder when we were, 388
Bot, good Ieuan, nowe praye for me
That we to geder in blese maye be.'

COTTON

Allas! what is me to rede,
mi Muror is broken & is dede,
þat my likynge was Inne. 537
Hope of ioie nou haue I loren,
& serwe is newed me beforen
þat neuermore schal blinne.' 540

Al þe folk þat stod be-side,
þat seiȝ heore serwe so vnride,
a wepten ful tenderliche. 543
þer was non þat miȝte hem holde,
Mon ne wommon, ȝong ne olde,
and þat was no feorliche. 546

VERNON

// Allas! what is me to rede?
Mi mirour is broken & is dede
þat my liking was Inne. 537
hope of ioye now haue I lorn,
& sorwe is newed me be-forn
þat neuere more schal blynne." 540

// Al þat folk þat stod be-syde,
þat say þe sorwe so vn-ruyde,
þey wepe ful tendreliche; 543
þer ne was non þat myȝtte him holde,
Man ne wif man, ȝung ne old;
& þat nas no ferliche. 546

LAUD 108

// 'Allas, þat' I. was woman bore,
Nou .I. haue þe forlore,
My leof' so hende. 549
Sorwefulliche me is dyght',
Nou þou wiþ me speke ne myht,
I. ne recke whider to wende.' 552

// vp she stod' beforn hem alle,
to drouh hir' heer & hir' calle,
as she were feye. 555
Bitter teres she let' falle,
for hire þei wer' sory alle,
þat' hir' wepe seye. 558

LAUD 463

[1]¶ A-wey, þat ich was woman y-bore,
Now ich haue þe for-lore, [1 leaf 77]
My leman so hende. 549
Sorweful is me y-diȝt,
Now þou with me speke ne myȝt,
Ne reiche ich whyder to wende." 552

¶ Of hy stod by-fore hem alle,
To-drouȝ here her, and here calle,
As hy were veiȝe. 555
Bytere teres hy let falle,
ffor hire were sory alle,
þat here wepe y-seiȝe. 558

TRINITY

(92)

¶ þapostoile & þe clergie,
þemperoures & her chiualerie,
Token þat confessoure,   1095
And leiden on a bere riȝth;
ffair & wel hij habbeþ hym diȝth,
wiþ menske & honoure;   1098

LAUD 622

To þe chirche of seint Bonefas,
wiþ þe corps þai token þe pas
wiþouten any soioure;   1101
þe belles alle aȝein hem rungen,
Preostes & clerkes merily sungen
wiþ þat swete floure.   1104

LAUD 622

The folke come fast owte of þe cete,   that ryche Relyke for to see.   392

COTTON   COTTON

¶ þe pope¹ com, & þe Emperours
bad bringe him forþ out of þe hous
& lei him on A bere, [¹ pope crosst through]
And bar him wiþ solempnete,
forþ Amidde þe cite,
& criȝinge þat almiȝte here,   552
And seide, 'come seoþ þat holi mon
þat ȝe haue souȝt euerichon,
here he is in þis place.   555
He is founden, and he is here,
þat holi bodi on a beere,
þorwh help of godus grace.'   558

VERNON

// þe pope com forþ, & te Emperours
Leten him bringe owt of þe hous,   549
& leyden him on a bere,
And beren wiþ gret solempnete
In-to þe mydeward of þe cyte,
& cryeden þat alle myȝten here,   552
& seyden: "comeþ, seþ þis holyman
þat ȝe han south euerichon!
here he is in þis place;   555
ffounden he is, & is here,
þat holy body on a bere,
þoru help of godes grace."   558

LAUD 108

¶ So mychel sorwe þer was,
Bot who-so hadde a tong⸵ of bras
ne myghte it al telle.   561
þe day was almest⸵ do,
þe pope & þemperour also
Might no lenger dwelle.   564
þat liche þei let wake & shride,
wiþ pal & wiþ oþer pride,
þat þei founde þere.   567
wiþ michel ioye & hey song⸵,
þe bisshopes hem alle among⸵
þe corps to chirche bere.   570
// Amydde ryght⸵ þe heye strete
So mychel folk⸵ þei gonne mete
þat þei most⸵ astonde.   573
¶ Alle seke þat to him come
y-helede were .y.-lome
Of feet⸵ & of honde.   576

LAUD 463

¶ So moche sorwe þer was,
Bote who-so hadde a tonge of bras,
Ne myȝte he it telle.   561
þe day him was al-mest y-do,
þe Pope and þe emperour al-so
Ne myȝte lenger dwelle.   564
¶ þat lich hy lete by-wake, and shrude
With palle and with oþer prude,
þat hy founde þere.   567
With mochel liȝt, and mochel song⸵,
þat holy cors hem alle among⸵,
Bischoppis to cherche bere.   570
¶ Amyddes riȝt þe heȝe strete,
So moche folk⸵ hy gonne mete,
þat hy resten a stounde.   573
Alle þe sike þat to him come,
I-heled were swiþe sone,
Of fet and ek of honde.   576

TRINITY

(93)

¶ Noman may telle wiþ tunge	Men þat weren in palesye,
þe miracles þat of hym sprunge	Lunatik', oiþer in frenesie,
As þai þat body bere; 1107	Bote hadden þere. 1113
Deef' & doumbe, halte & blynde,	Swiche presse was þe poeple among',
Alle miȝtten bote fynde,	þemperoures miȝtten nouȝth for þrong'
In maladie þat were; 1110	Beren forþ þe bere. 1116
LAUD 622	LAUD 622
Sone in a A lytell stonde þer was	Bothe grete throng And prece.
COTTON	COTTON

Alle þat wusten of þat cri,	// Alle þat wisten of þat cry,
þei ornen þidere wel hasteli,	þei ronne þider hastifly,
þei tolde þeron nout a lyte. 561	& ne drou it nowt to abyd. 561
An Alle þe seke þat þer were,	And alle þe sike þat þer were,
þat miȝte touche þat bodi þere,	þat myȝtte touche þe body þere,
þei weren hole as tite. 564	þei were hol als tyd. 564
þe blinde hedde þere of him here siȝt,	// þe blynde, of him hadden here syȝth;
woode of him heore wit fol riȝt,	þe wode, here wyth hadde ful ryȝth;
þe halt here limes hole Anon. 567	þe halte, here lymes lele. 567
Hit was non þat þider miȝte winne,	þer ne was non þat þider myȝte wynne,
what seknes þei were inne,	What syknesse þat þei were Inne,
þat þei were hole vchon. 570	þat þei ne hadde here hele. 570
VERNON	LAUD 108

// þe blynde come to her' sight',	¶ þe blynde come to har' siȝt,
þe crokede gonne to righte,	þe crokede gonne sone riȝt,
þe lame to go; 579	þe lame for to go; 579
þat doumbe wer' fonge speche,	þat dombe were fenge speche,
þei heried' god, þe soþe leche,	þeȝ herede god, þe soþe leche,
& þe halwe also. 582	And þat halwe al-so. 582
// þe day ȝeode & drouh to nyȝht,	¶ þe day ȝede, and drouȝ to-nyȝt,
No lenger dwelle þei ne myght',	No lenger dwelle hy ne myȝt,
to chirche þei most' wend. 585	To cherche hy moste wende; 585
þe bellen begonne to rynge,	þe bellen hy gonne to rynge,
þe clerkes forto singe,	þe clerkes heȝe to synge,
Euerich in his ende. 588	Euerich in his ende. 588
¶ þo þei to þe chirche cam,	¶ þo þe cors to cherche com,
Glad þei were eche of ham	Glad hy were euerichon,
þat þer-inne were. 591	þat þer-ynne were. 591
þe pope & þemperour	þe Pope and þe emperour,
before þe auter of seint sauour	By-fore an auter of seint sauour,
sette þe bere. 594	¶ þer sette hy þe bere. 594
LAUD 463	TRINITY

(94)

¶ þai biþouȝtten hem in þis wyse,
þat folk⁰ was ful of Coueitise,
And tresore onon of sende, 1119
And casten aboute siluer & golde,
Take it vp who þat wolde,
Largely to spende. 1122
LAUD 622

Nouȝth for þan in euery strete
þe presse was swiþe grete,
þai miȝtten hem nouȝth defende; 1125
þai leten lygge þat tresoure,
And foloweden þat confessoure
þat day to þe ende. 1128
LAUD 622

The emperoure, that stode þer þoo,
Sawe þe folke presyd ssoo; 396
Sylvyr in þe strete þey cast,
To lete the folke þat com so Fast,
Bot of sylver yaffe þey no force,
Alle held hem Fast to se þat corce.
COTTON

At þe last with trawayle borne hyt
was 401
To þe chyrche of seynt bonyfface.
whan yt was to þe chyrche I-brought,
A ryche tombe þere was wrought,
Of marbyll And of ryche stonys,
COTTON

¶ whon þe Emperours sai þe wonder
þei toke þe bere & eode þer-vndur,
with the Pope¹ helpande; [¹ crosst out]
ffor þei wolde be i-mad holi,
þorwh beringe of þat bodi,
þei toke þe bere in hande. 576

þei made sowen in þat cite
gold & seluer gret plente;
and þat was for þis skil 579
þat þe folk scholde hem with-drawe,
and þat auayled not worþ an haue,
þei tok no tent þer-til. 582
VERNON

//Whan þe emperour him say þat won-
he¹ tok þe bere & ȝide þer-vnder, [der,
Wiþ þe pope he wende, [¹ MS. ho].
ffor he wolde ben mad holy
þoru þe bering of þat body,
he tok þe bere in hande. 576

// he let sowe in þe cyte
Gold & siluer gret plente,
& þat was for þis skyl, 579
ffor þe folk scholde hem wiþdrawe;
bote þat a-vaillede nat an hawe,
þey toke no tent þer-til. 582
LAUD 108

// Aboute þe ber' was mychel lyght',
wiþ fair pal it was betyght',
& wiþ cloþes of golde. 597
fforto honour' þis holy man,
of al þat lond folk⁰ þider cam,
þat fayn wake wolde. 600

// Alle seke þat þere were,
As sone as þei turned þe bere,
hole þei were anon 603
Of þe yuel þat þei hedde,
If þei in þe nome bede
of þis holy mon. 606
LAUD 463

A-boute þe bere was moche liȝt;
With proude palle was be-diȝt,
I-beten al with golde. 597
ffor to worschipe þis man,
Al þat lond folk⁰ þuder cam,
þat cors by-wake wolde. 600

¶ Alle þe sike þat þer were,
As sone as hy touchede þe bere,
Hol hy were anon 603
Of þe euel þat hy hadde,
ȝif hy in þe name badde
Of þis holy man. 606
TRINITY

(95)

¶ Ri3th at seint Bonefas chirche,	His fader / his moder / & his wijf,
To seint Alexi þai gonne wirche	Lyueden after in holy lijf·
A riche monument : 1131	Trewely wiþ gode entent·. 1137
Seuene dayes his frendes duelleden	And whan þai dyeden alle þre,
ffor his body þat lay on bere, [þere	þai wenten wiþ solempnite
And siþens hom þai went. 1134	To god omnipotent·. 1140
LAUD 622	LAUD 622

Craffetyly, And for þe nonce,	And other man many And fette :
of sylvyr And of golde coloure,	Thorowe grace of god þey hadden hell.
They layd in þys Ryche tresowre.	Be thys holy man men may ssee,
Sythen cam on to hys tombe 409	That god lowyght wele pouerte ;
Blynde And lame, dethe And dome,	he for soke thys worlde all bedene,
	And lowyd god, And yt ys sene
COTTON	COTTON

þei preced euer neer and neere,	þei preceden euere ner & nerre,
forte come to þat bere	fforto comen to þe bere
þat þe cors lay Inne. 585	þat þe corps lay Inne ; 585
þei precede wiþ so gret fors	þei preseden þerto wiþ gret fors,
þat vnneþe with þe holi cors,	þat vnneþe wiþ þat holy cors
to chirche mi3te þei winne. 588	To churche my3te þei wynne. 588
¶ whon þei come to þe chirche,	// Whanne þei comen to þe churche,
A toumbe of gold þei lette worche	A toumbe of gold he leten wurche
of preciouse stones. 591	Wiþ preciouse stones ; 591
In A schort tyme hit was diht,	In seue dayes it was dy3th
ful richeliche and Al ari3t	fful richeliche al a-ry3th,
þei leide þer-in his bones. 594	þei leyden þer-inne þe bones. [leaf 237]
VERNON	LAUD 108

¶ To chirche com 3ong· & olde,	¶ To cherche come 3onge & olde,
þat holy corps to beholde,	þat holy cors to by-holde
þat þider was .y.-brought. 609	þat þuder was y-bro3t. 609
A wel gentyl marbelston,	A wel gentel marbel ston,
To louke inne his holy bon,	To louke in his holy bon,
Sone was y.-sought. 612	Sone was by-so3t. 612
þe thridde day was .y.-come,	¶ þe þridde day was y-come,
So me dide þe londes wone,	So it is þe londis wone,
Men dide þe seruise. 615	Me dude þe seruyse ; 615
þeder· com more & lasse,	þuder come more and lasse,
þe pope self song· þe masse,	þe Pope self song þe masse,
wiþ-outen feyntise. 618	With herte wel blyþe. 618
LAUD 463	TRINITY

(96)	In þe worschip of god in glorie,
¶ þus ende & orde ȝee han yherd,	Out of latyn is drawen þis storie,
Of seint Alexi hou it ferd,	þorouȝ miȝth of heuene kyng. 1146
wiþouten any lesyng. 1143	alle þat habben yherd his vye,
LAUD 622	LAUD 622
he for soke hys Fader, Moder, And wyffe, 417	And lyvyd A pore manys lyfe; Nowe is he in Ioye þat last[et]he Aye.
COTTON	COTTON
whon þat holi cors was leid	Wan þat holy cors was leyd
in þat toumbe þat wel was greiþed,	In-to þe toumbe richeliche I-greyþud
wiþ ful gret honour, 597	Wiþ ful meche honour: 597
To alle þat weren in þat place	To alle þat were in þat place
þer com out, þorwh godes grace,	þer com owt þoru godes grace
a ful swete odour; 600	A ful swete odour. 600
So swote felede þei neuer non,	So swete ne smelde þei neuere non,
as wyde as þei hedden gon,	Als so wyde as þey hadden gon,
of no spicerie. 603	Of no spiserye. 603
VERNON	LAUD 108
þo þe masse was y.-do,	¶ þo þe masse was y-do,
þe pope & þemperour also,	þe Pope and þe emperour al-so,
þe holy corps þei kiste. 621	þat holy cors hy kiste. 621
þei nome þo þe holy bon,	Hy nome þe holy man, [leaf 77, back]
& leide it in a marbelston,	And leyde him in þe marbel ston,
y-loke in a chiste. 624	By-loke in one chiste. 624
¶ Alle þilk þat þer' were,	¶ Alle þulke þat þer were,
heried god wiþ loude bere,	Herede god with loude bere,
& crieden mercy, 627	And cride him mercy, 627
LAUD 463	TRINITY

God brynge hem to þe compaignye
þere Aungels ben wonyynge; 1149
And sende vs, lorde, þi mylde
  mood;

LAUD 622

ffor þorouȝ þee spryngeþ al good
wiþouten any endynge. 1152
  Amen, Amen, Amen.

LAUD 622

God bryng us þere þat best maye.
Praye wee All þat yt soo bee. 421

COTTON

Amen, Amen, For cheryte.
  explicit sante alex.

COTTON

þenne worschupeden heo Alle with o
  steuene,
Iesu, godus sone of heuene,
and his Modur Marie. 606
Iesu crist, þorwh þe preiȝere
of him þat we haue of told here,
ȝif þi wille hit be, 609
Graunt vs alle god endyng,
and in heuene a wonyng.
AMEN par Charite. 612

VERNON

þei worchipeden him alle wiþ o
  stephne
& þankeden Iesu crist of heuene
& his moder Marye. 606
// Nou Iesu crist þoru þe preyer
of þat cors seint I tolde ȝou her,
ȝif þi wille it be, 609
Graunte vs alle god endyng,
And in heuene a wonying! 612
Amen, par charite.

LAUD 108

Of þe wonder þat he dide
In þe selue holy stede,
ffor loue of Alexij. 630
¶ Beseke we ȝerne & ofte, [leaf 118, bk]
Ihesu þat vs deore boughte,
þat he vs grace sende. 633
þat we mote him seruy,
And for þe loue of Alexij,
To his blisse wende. AMEN. 636

LAUD 463

Of þe wondres þat he dude
þo in þat ilke holy stude,
ffor loue of allexi. 630
¶ By-seche we þanne, ȝerne & ofte,
Crist self þat vs dere boȝte,
þat his grace vs sende, 633
þat we mote him seruy,
And for þe loue of allexi,
To his blesse wende. Amen. 636

TRINITY

King Solomon's Book of Wisdom,

A BOOK OF MORAL PRECEPTS AND PRACTICAL ADVICE
(lines 1—105),

Taken from the Laud MS. 622's headless rymed Bible Story, and follow'd by the end of that Story, an account of

1. King SOLOMON'S love of Lechery, p. 85, l. 107—111. (For his Coronation, his Judgment on the Child claimd by 2 Mothers, and his Wisdom, &c., see p. 96-8);
2. of his son REHOBOAM, l. 113—131; and the separation of the Kingdoms of Judah and Israel, 132—146; p. 85-86;
3. legends of the prophet ELIJAH, 150; his raising the prophet Jonah[1] (the widow of Zarephath's son, 1 Kings xvii. 17) to life, 156-65; going to Horeb, 166-73; his choosing Elisha, 174-7; burning up king Ahaziah's messengers (2 Kings i. 10—12), 178—199; and going to heaven in a fiery horse and cart (2 Kings ii. 11), 200—213; p. 86-88;
4. of ELISHA, his purifying a well with salt, 214—225 (2 Kings ii. 19-22); and multiplying a poor woman's oil, 226—233 (2 Kings iv. 1—3); p. 88;
5. of DANIEL in the lions' den, fed with Abacuc's food, 234—263; and of Apostles and Friars preaching Christianity, 264-7; p. 88-89;
6. of the *Day of Doom*, 268; and herein, p. 89-90;
7. of ANTICHRIST, 272; how he shall go into the Holy Land, 274; slay Enoch and Eli, who have come to earth from Paradise to fight him, 292-6; and shall then himself be smitten to death by the Holy Ghost in the form of a sword.

All in alternate fours and threes[2], the latter ryming. In the rymes the equivalence of final 'ȝth' with 'ȝt' is to be noted[3],—l. 52, 51, 71-2; (but see 57-8, 7-8, 19-24, 33-4, &c.),—and these forms and rymes: *prep.* mytte (with), wytte, 43-4; but 'myde', iryde (ridden), 249-50; erþe, fierþe (fourth), 99-100; mesure, here, 89-90; consaile (*obl.*), availe (*inf.*), 115-16; but conseil (*obj.*), israel, 141-2; seiȝe (3 *pl. perf.* saw), diȝe (*inf.* die), 191-2; but 'seiȝ', on heiȝ (high), 201-2; pite (put, ? *inf., imp.,* or *subj.*), a 'lite' (little), 225-6; ydytte (*pp.* of dihtan, see 254) 'pytte' (pit), 241-2; vchone, fon, 262-3. The *ie* is right: folie, wrie (*inf.*), 79-80; Elye, prophecie, 152-3, &c. The final *e* can hardly be allowd to þing (*obl.*) to match springe (*inf.*), 3-4 (see 59-60); cp. telle, well, 55-6. Mowe, abouȝe, 27-8, seem to show the silence of ȝ. There are two 'longe' s probably of the same meaning ryming, 91-2. The ryming of 'ysed' (*pp.*) with 'ded' (dead, *pp.*), 195-6; of 'sede' (*perf.*) with 'falshede', 266, and the six '-ede' words in 267-272 (*drede* among them); of 'seide' with 'rede', 179-180, shows that the Elizabethan and our 'sed' is not, as has been asserted, a mere late slurring of the broad 'said', tho' that form or spelling has won in the fight for the survival of the fittest.

---

[1] That Jonah was the son of the widow of Zarephath is in the Midrash Yalqût (a legendary Commentary on the Old Testament, called Yalqût) to the book Jonah, quoted from the Talmud of Jerusalem.—A. Neubauer.
[2] A few fours, as 183, 202, 207, are but three measures; while a few threes, as 234 and 244, are fours.
[3] Cp. *Havelok*, fiht, rith, 2716; with, knith = wiht, knight, 2720.—Skeat.

[Laud MS. 622, leaf 69, back.]

Proem.
Solomon's every word was wisdom.

SO mychel wisdom neuer y-herd was ⸵ as kyng salamon couþe ⸵
 Vche word wyt & wisdom was ⸵ þat com out of his mouþe.
Þe kynde he couþe of vche beest ⸵ & of vche quik þing,
And þe vertu of vche herbe ⸵ þat doþ on erþe spr[i]nge ;   4
And þorouȝ queintise in book ywrite ⸵ þe fende to ouer-come,
þat þise clerkes ȝutt to þis day ⸵ in priuete habbeþ some.

I. Solomon's Book of Wisdom. He made a Book of Wisdom. I'll give you part of it.

A Book he made of wisdom ⸵ þorouȝ his owen þouȝth ;
 Sum ich wil þerof telle ⸵ for al ne may I nouȝth.   8
 Þe book bigan in þis manere ⸵ euerich wyt & wisdom,
Euer with oure lord it is ⸵ & fro hym first it com.
Who schulde þe rein-dropes telle ⸵ oiþer þe grauel in þe Cee,
Oiþer þe dayes þat euere were ⸵ bot ȝif it were he ?   12

Fear of God is wisdom's root.

To douten god almiȝtty ⸵ of vche wisdom it is rote.
On erþe & at þine endyngday ⸵ of alle bales he is bote.
Ȝif þou louest wisdom ⸵ look þou riȝth loue ⸵
Vnbuxum ne be þou nouȝth ⸵ to þem þat ben þe aboue.   16

Help the needy.

Helpe þe man þat nedeful is ⸵ be aȝeins hym þat is vnmylde.
Be þou merciable to widewe ⸵ & to faderles childe.
Ne hide nouȝth þi wisdom ⸵ ne wiþseie nouȝth þe riȝth.

Don't fight strong and wrathful men.

Aȝein stronge men & ireful ⸵ look þat þou ne fiȝth.   20
Answere þe pouere myldelich ⸵ to longe abid þou nouȝth
Forto turne aȝein to god ⸵ ȝif þou be in synne brouȝth.

Cease not to work and fight to sustain the right.

// Ne bileue þou nouȝth to trauaile ⸵ oiþer to deþ[e] fiȝth,
For Iesu cristes swete loue ⸵ to susteyne þe riȝth.   24
Wiþ þe fole ne wone þou nouȝth ⸵ ȝif þou wilt good lerne.
Þou wisse hym þat litel good can ⸵ þe vnwise teche ȝerne.

Don't be a Justice unless you're fit for one.

Ne wilne nouȝth Iustise to be ⸵ bot ȝif þou cunne & mowe.
Þe vnbuxum, chastise wiþ riȝth lawȝe ⸵ & make þe proude abouȝe.

þei3 þou haue a .M. frendes ⁘ take on þat be good & priuee,　　　　Have 1 good friend.
þat þou mowe þi conseil telle ⁘ lest' þe oþer failen þe.　　30
For summe ben at' þi borde þi frende ⁘ ac at' þi nede bihynde.
Best' tresore is þine elde frende ⁘ þat men on erþe may fynde;　　An old friend is the best
þi trewe frende emforþ þi-self' ⁘ þou mi3th telle þi þou3th;　33　treasure on earth.
Michel solas he wil þe don ⁘ 3if þou art in baret' brou3th.
¶ To Newfangel ne be þou nou3th ⁘ lest þou finde vntrewe.
þine olde frende þat þou fonded haste ⁘ bileue þou for no newe.
Faire speche is [ful] good þing' ⁘ it passeþ many fon,　　37　Fair speech beats many
And makeþ many a good frend ⁘ & holdeþ hol many a bon.　　foes.
Chese þe a witty hyne ⁘ & loue hym with al þi mi3th;
Of his Salerie wiþholde þou nou3th ⁘ þat þou schalt hym with
　　ri3th.
þerwhile þi sones 3onge beþ ⁘ þou hem chastise & lere;　　41　Thrash and teach your
Wite þi douttren with eye wel ⁘ þat þai haue of þe fere;　　young sons. [Ecclus. xxx.
Selde þou make hem fair semblaunt ⁘ þerwhile þai ben þe mytte;　1, 10.] Seldom smile
Whan þai schullen ywedded be ⁘ take hem a man of wytte.　44　at your daughters.
// Honoure fader & moder ⁘ þat þe in-to þis werlde brou3th;　　Honour your father and
þe pyne þat þi moder had ⁘ haue it mychel in þou3th.　　mother.
Who so honoureþ fader & moder ⁘ þe lenger he worþe alyue;
His hous & al his erþlich þing' ⁘ þe better schal yþriue.　　48
To þe seke gladlich þou go ⁘ þan doostou as þe kynde.
In euerych dede þat þou doost' ⁘ þine endynge haue in mynde.
¶ Ne chide nou3th wiþ no foule speker ⁘ with riche ne plede　Don't go to law with
　　þou no3t';　　rich men
For oft' þe ri3th, þorou3 gret' mede ⁘ is in-to wrong' y-brou3th. 52　They bribe.
Mid a fole, of þi þing' ⁘ ne make þou non In mone.　　Don't share your goods
Wiþ a Man þat fool-hardy is ⁘ ne goo þou nou3th alone.　　with a fool.
To fool ne to non vncouþ man ⁘ þi conseil [þou] ne telle, [col. 2]
For þe fool, bot' his foly ⁘ noþing' ne loueþ wel.　　56
Ne biholde no faire wymmen ⁘ þat þai ne chaunge þi þou3t';
Ne loue no womman with þine hert' ⁘ þat sche ne gile þe nou3t';　Don't love any woman,
Ne biholde nou3th in þe strete ⁘ aboute fram þing' to þing'.　for fear she'll trick you.
3if a liþer man doþ þe vnri3th ⁘ ne haue þerof no likyng'.　60
Dele þi frendes & pouere men ⁘ þi good by þi daye;　　Give your money away
Ne bileue it nou3th to oþer men ⁘ lest þai þe bitraye.　　while you live.

Don't have many children.	Ne delite þe nouȝth to gete children ⸵ many & vnmylde,	
	ffor ȝutᵗ þe were betterᵗ ⸵ to deye wiþouten childe.	64
	¶ Amended is al a cuntre ⸵ wiþ a Man þat is wys.	
	And for a liþer man ⸵ mychel enpaired I-wis.	
Ware taverns and Lechery.	A riche werkᵗ of dronkelew man ⸵ selde is yfounde,	
	For Tauerne & leccherie ⸵ many man bringeþ to grounde	68
Keep your secrets to yourself.	Noiþer þi frende ne þi foo ⸵ ne telle þou þi priuete;	
	For botᵗ he be þe better frendᵗ ⸵ ȝif he wotᵗ any yuel by þe	
	þat þou ne most þe more hym bowȝe ⸵ ȝif þou misseist hym ouȝt,	
	þat yuel þat he wotᵗ by þe ⸵ he nyll it hele nouȝth.	72
Reprove your friend if he does wrong, unless he's a fool.	Vndernyme þi frendᵗ ⸵ ȝif þou seest hym mysdo;	
	Ȝif he is a fool or þi foo ⸵ ne do þou nouȝth so.	
	Riche ȝiftes & presentȝ ⸵ maken þise Iuges blynde,	
	Þat þai cunnen yse þe riȝth ⸵ þe wrongᵗ sone þai fynde.	76
	// wisdom yheled, litel is worþ ⸵ oiþer treuþ ihydᵗ;	
	Botᵗ boþe þai wexen swiþe ⸵ ȝif þai ben y-kydᵗ.	
Show wisdom. Hide folly.	Good is, wisdom to schewe ⸵ & to hely folie;	
	For þe fool ne can hele noþingᵗ ⸵ botᵗ he itᵗ outᵗ wrie;	80
	His hertᵗ is as a vessel ⸵ þat boþome ne haþ non;	
	Whan any þingᵗ þerinne comeþ ⸵ it goþ outᵗ onon.	
How to know a fool: he's a runabout, eaves-dropper, and liar.	A fool, men mowen wel yknowe ⸵ for oftᵗ he goþ aboute	
	With erandes to many hous ⸵ & oftᵗ he stant wiþoute,	84
	And goþ to a windowe stillelich ⸵ & softᵗ lokeþ þer-inne,	
	Oiþer herkneþ þerat what men ⸵ seien þere wiþinne.	
	Sone & lovde he wil liȝe ⸵ whan he hereþ foly telle:	87
	A wise man wolde aschamed be ⸵ ȝif swich a cas hym bifelle.	
	Vche wordᵗ þat atᵗ his mouþe schal come, schal be by mesure;	
	Hym is loþ to telle myche ⸵ ac leue myche to here.	90
3 wisdoms.	Ȝutᵗ þre wisdoms lerne of me ⸵ ne þenche nouȝth to longe;	
	Be nouȝth sory for no los ⸵ ne after noþingᵗ longe,	92
	Namelich þat þou ne miȝth nouȝth haue ⸵ ne nouȝth þerfore ne care.	
	Ne al þat þou herestᵗ, ne leue þou nouȝth ⸵ ȝif þou wilt wel fare.	
The good of teaching.	An vntauȝtᵗ childe his fader schent more ⸵ þan þei hem selue don;	
	Þe man þat techeþ his children wel ⸵ sore saweþ his fon.	96
3 things on earth no man can know.	Þre þinges on erþe beþ ⸵ þat men mowen nouȝth y-knowe:	
	Whiche hij ben, I schal ȝou telle ⸵ boþe to heiȝe & lowe:	

þe fissches weie in þe Cee ! þe snakes weie on erþe,
And þe foules waie in þe sky ! þe werst is þe fierþe : 100 *The 4th and worst: to let a child have its will.*
þat is, childes waie in his ȝouþe ! ȝif it haþ his wille.
For many a foule waie it will goo ! & selde sittᵗ stille.
þis bookᵗ made Salamon ! of þise wisdoms & more : [leaf 70] *End of Solomon's*
To mychel he loued leccherie ! for al his wise lore, 104 *Book of Wisdom.*
Seuenty wyues in spousehode ! he helde al his lyfᵗ, *He had 70 wives and*
And þre hundreþ in leccherie ! þat non þerof was his wyfᵗ. *300 concubines.*
Fourty wyntren he was kyng ! & died in þe fourtide ȝere.
Telle men miȝtten þat he were safᵗ ! ȝif leccherie nere. 108 *His lechery may have*
Foure hundreþ ȝer & seuentene ! it was þo he died, & mo, *damnd him.*
þat þe folkᵗ of Israel ! outᵗ of Egipte gunnen go.

Affter kyngᵗ Salomons deþ ! Roboam his sone *II. Of Rehoboam.*
Was of þat londe kyngᵗ ymade ! as it was þe wone. 112 *Rehoboam his son reignd in his*
þat folkᵗ cried on hym a day ! þat he a-legge scholde *stead.*
þe seruage þat his fader hem made ! þe better serue hym þai *When his folk askt him*
wolde. *to lighten their serfage,*
þerfore with alle his olde men ! þe kyngᵗ went to conseile : 115
þai radden hym mylde forto be ! þe more it wolde hym availe.
He cleped forþ his ȝonge folkᵗ ! as he hym selfᵗ was, *he followd*
& axed wheþer þe reed was goodᵈ ! þai seiden þat it nas ; *his young friends'*
Botᵗ " be þou sterne & dredeful ! & þan wil þai ben goodᵈ ; 119 *advice,*
Ne schaltou hem neuere good holde ! botᵗ with sterne moodᵈ."
¶ þe kyngᵗ þis conseil loued wel ! his bondemen he lete fecche. *and told his bondmen*
"Wene ȝe for my fader was wys ! þat ich wil be a wrecche.
In þe leftᵗ fynger þat ich haue ! strengþe þere is more 123 *that his left finger should*
þan was in al my fader schulder ! for al his wise lore *be heavier than his*
Ȝif he ȝou brouȝth in seruage ! to more I wil ȝou drawe. *father's shoulder*
Wene ȝe þeiȝ ich be ȝongᵗ ! þat ich ne couþe ȝou lawe ? " *(1 Kings xii.*
þis folkᵗ crieden ȝerne & wepen ! sore þai hem draddᵈ ; *10–14).*
Ac for noþingᵗ þai miȝtten do ! oþer wordᵈ þai naddᵈ. 128

Po þai weren from hym ywent ! gret conseil þai token. *So the 10 tribes of*
þe ten kyndes of israel ! for kyngᵗ þai hym forsoken, *Israel chose them a new*
And made hem a newe kyngᵗ ! ne stode hem of hym non *king (Jeroboam),*
eie ;
ffor þere ne leued wiþ hym ! bot þe kyndes tweie, 132 *and left Rehoboam only 2 tribes,*

Bot þe kynde of Beniamyn ⸭ & þe kynde of Iudas;
Alle þe kyndes of þe oþer ten ⸭ aʒeins hym fast was.
þe kyngˀ sent messagers to hem ⸭ & gret doel to hym he
 nom;

and stoned his messengers (Adoniram, 1 Kings xii. 18).

Wiþ stones þai slowʒen his messagers ⸭ þat to hem from hym
 com.   136

After þai maden Ieroboam kyng ⸭ wel he gan hem paie;
 And euere þe kyngdom departed is ʒutˀ to þis daye.
 þe kyngdom of þe tweie kyndes ⸭ Iudee ycleped is;
þerinne oure lord was ybore ⸭ in Bethleem iwis.   140

Jeroboam's kingdom of 10 tribes is calld Israel.

þe kyngdom of þe ten kyndes ⸭ ycleped is israel;
þere miʒth Roboam þe kyngˀ ⸭ acursy fole conseil.
Ofte eye & pride, harme doeþ ⸭ þere men miʒth yse;

No man can stand alone.

So riche a man in londe nis ⸭ þat mowe al-one be;   144
So riche a kyngˀ in þe werlde nys ⸭ þat poure begger he nere,
ffor al þe richesse þat he haþ ⸭ ʒif vche man his fo were.

III. Of Elijah.

IT bifel in israel ⸭ by þe kyngesday, swiche a cas:
 þere was a wise prophete ⸭ Elye ycleped he was.   148
 In wildernesse he woned ⸭ þe good prophete Elye,
 ffor þe kyngˀ awaited hym to sle ⸭ for his prophecie.

He dwelt in the desert for fear of King Ahab; and a raven fed him (1 Kings xvii.).

A morewen & an euen a Rauen ⸭ þere com vche a day,
And brouʒth þe prophete mete ⸭ in wildernesse þere he lay. 152
Siþen as oure lorde hym hete ⸭ to a toun he wende,
And seiʒ a widewe gadre wood ⸭ onon to hir he kende.

He raised to life the widow of Zarepheth's son, who was afterwards the prophet Jonah, and was sent to preach against Niniveh.

þere he woned longe wiþ hire ⸭ a day þer fel a cas
þat þe widewe son died ⸭ he was yhote Ionas;   156
Elie arered hym fram deþ to lyue ⸭ þorouʒ goddes sonde;
And siþen he was a prophete ⸭ þe wisestˀ in þe londe.
ffor wel longe afterward ⸭ oure lord bad Ionas gon
To þe Cite of Niniue ⸭ þat schulde haue ben fordon   160
ffor synne þat þai hadden ydon ⸭ Ionas was adrad,
Ac forto prechen þider he ʒede ⸭ as oure lord hym bad.

Elijah was 40 days at Horeb without food (1 Kings xix. 8).

// To þe hil of Oreb ⸭ Ely redy wende
þere Moyses in þe brennyngˀ þorne ⸭ oure lorde kende: 164
ffourty dayes he was þiderward ⸭ þat he ne ete ne dronkˀ
As it goddes will was ⸭ he had mychel þonkˀ.

þere oure lorde spak' wiþ hym : & hete hym good lyf lede,
And wende aȝein to israel : & noþing' ne drede. 168
" // A Man þat hatte Elisee : by þe waie þou schalt' fynde ; *God bade him*
þou schalt' hym take forþ wiþ þe : þat he ne leue bihynde." *take Elisha with him.*
Elie þe prophete went forþ : til he in-to desert cam. 171
He fonde Elyse gon on þe pleyn : with hym forþ he hym nam *They go to the land of*
To þe londe of¹ israel¹ : þai nadden of þe kyng' non eye. *Israel.*
Elise fonde anoþer prophete : & þider þai wenten beie.
þo lay þe kyng' sore seek' : & þo it was hym ysed, *King Ahaziah is sick,*
Elye tolde his messagers : þat he schulde be ded. 176
He hete his men wende after hym : þat þai sparen ne scholde ; *and sends his men after*
He wende, ȝif he miȝth hym haue hadd : þat he hym hele wolde. *Elijah (2 Kings i. 9).*
þei wenten forþ & comen to Elye : " goddes man " þai seide :
" þe kyng' hete þe come & speke with hym : ȝif þou couþest hym
    rede." 180

Elie seide " ȝif ich am goddes man : I. bid god al-one, *At Elijah's word,*
  þat wilde fire come fram heuen adoun : & brenne ȝou
    vchone."
Amyd þis word onon : fire fram heuen com, *fire from heaven burns*
And brent þise men al to dust' : þere was an hard dom. 184 *the men to dust.*
Sore alonged was þe kyng' : after hym ylome ;
Tueie he sent of oþer men : þo þai nouȝ[th] ne come. *Twice, other men of*
þai seiden as þe oþer deden : þo þai Elye seie ; *Ahaziah's are thus burnt*
And as þe oþer þai weren serued : ibrouȝth on liȝth leie. 188 *(2 Kings i. 11).*
þo þai ne comen nouȝth aȝein : þe kyng' þouȝth longe,
And lete sende after hym : wise men & stronge.
// Ȝerne þai crieden mercie : þo þai Elye seiȝe :
" Haue mercy on þe kyng' : or elles he schal diȝe." 192
þerof¹ seide Elye : " Siker he may be.
Ac, forto paye his corage : ich wil hym ones see."
Elye went' forþ to þe kyng' : & seide he schulde be ded ; *At last Elijah goes to the*
And sone he died þerafter-ward : as he had ysed. 196 *king; foretells his death; and*
Elie & Elisee in þe londe : wide aboute went', *he dies.*
For to tellen of prophecie : as oure lorde hem sent'.
As þai precheden goddes lawe : from heuen þere aliȝth
A fyry hors & a cart :—boþe þai weren wel briȝth ;— 200

¹ MS. isrk'.

88 KING SOLOMON'S BOOK OF WISDOM. IV. ELISHA. V. DANIEL.

Elijah goes up to heaven in a fiery horse-and-cart.

Elye þerinne went ⁚ þat hors hym drouȝ vp on heiȝ 201
In þe cartᵗ to heuen ⁚ þat men neuer eftᵗ hym ne seiȝ.
// Riȝth to heuen ne segge ich nouȝth ⁚ þat he euer come,

But he'll have to come back to earth on Dooms-Day,

For he schal haue fleschlich lyfᵗ ⁚ forto aȝeins þe day of dome.
We rede nouȝth botᵗ of two Men ⁚ þat hennes alyue went, 205
Enokᵗ & Elye ⁚ as god hem after sentᵗ.

that he and Enoch may fight Antichrist, and get kild.

Boþe þai wonen in paradys ⁚ & boþe þai schullen aliȝth
Aȝeins þe day of dome ⁚ & wiþ antecristᵗ fiȝth. 208
Anticrist hem schal boþe sle ⁚ & siþþen þai schullen wende
To þe blisse of heuen ⁚ & wonen þere wiþouten ende.

IV. *The Story of Elisha,*

DO Ely in þis fair cartᵗ ⁚ to heuen was yladᵈ,   **Elye** [lf 70, bk.]
Elisee his felawe ⁚ was sory, & nouȝth gladᵈ. 212
He ȝede to don his prophecie ⁚ in þe londe of Ierico :

Elisha finds a bad well in Jericho,

þere he fonde a liþer welle ⁚ þat many man dude wo,
ffor it wolde wex & sprede ⁚ wide & brode ilome,
Ne miȝth þe erþe bere no fruyt ⁚ þere þe water come. 216

and cures it by casting salt into it (2 Kings ii. 19—22).

þe prophete blissed saltᵗ ⁚ & in þe watere castᵗ;
þe liþerhede þat þerinne was ⁚ miȝth no lengere lastᵗ;
It bicom þe bestᵗ waterē ⁚ þat euer miȝth ben ;
Al þat it comeþ neiȝ ⁚ þe bettere schal þeen. 220

For this miracle, the priest puts salt to holy water.

ffor þe miracle þat men þo say ⁚ þat white saltᵗ had ydo,
Whan þe preest makeþ haliwater ⁚ saltᵗ he doþ þerto.

AWomman cried on Elisee ⁚ as sche hym mette,   **Eliseus**
& seide, men tookᵗ al hir goodᵈ ⁚ for hire hosebonde dette,
& þat sche naddᵈ nomore goodᵈ ⁚ botᵗ Oile alite. 225

Elisha multiplies the widow's oil (2 Kings iv. 1—8), so that she can pay her debts, and live.

Elisee badᵈ hire take þerof ⁚ & in vche vessel it pite
þat sche hadᵈ in al hire hous ⁚ & þo sche hadᵈ ydo þis,
Euerich vessel was ful ⁚ of goodᵈ oyle Iwis. 228
þis womman had þer þorouȝ ⁚ ynouȝ of al goodᵈ
fforto ȝelde her dettes ⁚ & to hire lyues foodᵈ.
Itᵗ bifel þat men of Babiloyne ⁚ weren of liþer bileue :
þai honoureden a fals god ⁚ a morewe & ekᵗ an eue. 232

V. *The Prophet Daniel.*

AWise prophete was in þat londe ⁚ þat hiȝth Danyel. ¶ **Danyel.**
He com & toldᵈ þe kyngᵗ 'fore ⁚ his men bileueden noȝtᵗ wel.
Ȝiue me power ouer hem ⁚ & ich hem wil bringe of dawe.'
þan seide þe kyngᵗ to hym ⁚ "þat were no wise lawe." 236

þat folk' þo þai herden þis ⸵ þe kyng' þai comen to : The Baby-
"ȝiue vs" þai seiden "Danyel ⸵ oure wiH with hym to do, lonians de-
Oiþer we schullen þe sle ⸵ er we hennes gon." mand Daniel
þe kyng' was of hem sore adrad' ⸵ & graunted' hem onon. 240 of their king,
Onon þai token Danyel þo ⸵ & casten hym in-to a pytte, and cast him
þere seuen hungri lyouns weren ⸵ þereinne aH ydytte, in a den of 7
ffor þai hym strangli scholden ⸵ ac þai deden hym non harme ; hungry lions.
Bot' whan þat he was sett' adoun ⸵ þai leneden in-to his barme. The lions
  Man þere was þat hiȝth Abacuc ⸵ in-to þe felde he went',* lan on
  Repmen forto bere mete ⸵ sone he hym þider sent'. *¶ Abacuk. Losom.
A þe Aungel hym bad' abide ⸵ & to Danyel it bere. 247 Abacuc re-
Sone he seide 'he nolde' ⸵ & ȝaf' hym liȝth ansuere. fuses to take
              Daniel food.
þe aungel took' hym by þe top ⸵ & bare hym forþ þer myde,— So an angel
Hym had' ben bettere to haue ygo ⸵ þan so fer to haue iryde,— picks him up
& so hym he bare to Danyel ⸵ & þo he com hym to, 251 by his top,
He ȝaf hym þe mete þat he bare ⸵ & lete Abacuc' go. gives Daniel
þo Danyel had' seueniȝth ⸵ ibe in þe dep pytt', his food, and
þe kyng' loked to his lyouns ⸵ & lete hem vndytt'. 254 drops Abacuc
¶ Alyue he fond' Danyel ⸵ gret' wonder he hadde. (*Bel and the*
Wiþ gret' ioye he took' hym vp ⸵ & to his fon hym lad'. *Dragon*,
þe men þat brouȝtten hym þere ⸵ he lete nyme fast', 33—39).
And euerych after oþere ⸵ amonge þe lyouns cast'. 258 The King
Sone hadden þe Lyouns ⸵ forswelewed' hem vchone ; takes Daniel
And so oure lorde euer among' ⸵ takeþ wreche of his fon. out of the
þapostles, forto þai weren yslawe ⸵ precheden cristendom ; den,
And many man after hem ⸵ good prechour bycom. 262 and casts his
And now þise freres don also ⸵ prechen aboute ylome, foes into it.
ffor of prechyng' it worþe nede ⸵ er þe day of dome. The Apostles
  E first signe þer aȝeins ⸵ as oure lord hym-self sede, preacht ; and
  Hungere schal on erþe be ⸵ treccherie & falshede, 266 so do the
Þ Batailes & litel loue ⸵ sekenesse & haterede ; Friars now ;
 & þe erþe schal quaken ⸵ þat vche man schal drede ; and they
 þe mone schal turne to blood ⸵ þe sunne to derk'hede ; need.
Antecrist' schal on erþe gon ⸵ & prechen his li er hede. VI. *The*
He schal go bot' in þe holy londe ⸵ þere oure lord' ȝede, *Signes o*"*the*
& his deciples in-to al þe werlde ⸵ his yuel wordes wil bede. *Day of Doom*.
              And herein
              VII. *Of Anti-*
              christ.
              He shall go
              into the Holy
              Land only.

His men shall do miracles, but not raise the dead.	As þai speken, þai schullen do ꞉ miracles grete & ryue ; Boþ' we ne fynde nouȝth þai mowe ꞉ arere þe ded to lyue. 274 Boþ' in-to cursed gostes ꞉ fendes willeþ go, fforto bere hem witnesse ꞉ of al þat he seiþ hem to.
Wise clerks shall withstand 'em.	þise grete clerkes & wise ꞉ aȝein hym schullen speke, fforto holden vp cristendom ꞉ þat men it nouȝth ne breke. 278
Fools say that clerks shall destroy this world.	Boþ' many of þise foles siggen ꞉ in her hastite, þat clerkes schullen fordo þis werld ꞉ boþ' so schal it noȝt' be, Boþ' þe fals clergie ꞉ þat antecrist' schal of preche ; 281 & fele þat in godenesse schulden be ꞉ liþer he wil hem teche. Ac so wys clerk' ne worþ þer non ꞉ þat ne schal haue to don ynouȝ fforto disputen aȝeins hym ꞉ þeiȝ he haue þe wouȝ.
Antichrist shall turn many to evil.	Many men schullen turne ꞉ to yuel, men may drede, 285 ffor on erþe men may se ꞉ to liþer, stedfast hede. Oure lord' leþ' hym on erþe gon ꞉ for þat he wil fonde Whiche men of stedfastnesse beþ ꞉ & cristendom vnderstonde.
Enoch and Elijah	Tueie men ben in paradys ꞉ Enok' & Elye ; 289 þai ne suffreden neuer deþ ꞉ as we han seid twie.
shall come down from heaven, fight Antichrist, and be slain.	Aȝeins þe day of dome ꞉ þai schullen on erþe aliȝth, And her eiþer after oþer ꞉ aȝeins Antecrist fiȝth. Anticrist' hem schal boþe sle ꞉ & fele Men willen þerfore 293 Turne to her bileue ꞉ & make her soules forlore.
The Holy Ghost shall kill Antichrist.	Atte last schal come þe holi gost' ꞉ in fourme of swerd' al[i]ȝt', & Anticrist' to deþ smyte ꞉ þorouȝ his swete miȝt. 296

St. Jeremie's 15 Tokens before Doomsday.

WITH

LAMENTACIO ANIMARUM,

WHAT OUR LORD SHALL DO AND SAY ON THAT DOOMSDAY; AND A SONG OF JOY AND BLISS, TO PRAISE THAT SWEET DEW, CHRIST.

(See other englisht copies of these '15 Tokens' attributed to St. Jerome, in my *Early English Poems* (Philolog. Soc. 1862), p. 7-12, and p. 162-4 (from *Metrical Homilies*, ed. Small, before publication); my *Hymns to the Virgin and Christ* (E. E. T. S., 1867), p. 118-125; Dr Morris's 'Hampole's *Pricke of Conscience*' (Philolog. Soc.), p. 135, l. 4738, &c, and *Cursor Mundi* (E. E. T. Soc.), p. 1282-1298, Part IV, and p. 1616-18 (from the Edinburgh MS), in the Appendix, Part V; Mr T. Wright's *Chester Plays* (copid by Geo. Bellin in 1592), vol. ii. 147-9; and in the same vol., p. 219-21 (from Harl. MS. 913, ab. 1309 A.D.), and p. 222-4 (from Harl. 2255); Mr Small's Northern '*Metrical Homilies*', p. 25-6, given also in Morris and Skeat's *Specimens of Early English*, 1298—1393, p. 83-5; Sir David Lyndesay's *Monarche*, book iv, l. 5462 (in Skeat's *Specimens*, 1394-1579, p. 254-6), &c, &c, &c. Old Friesic has a version of these 15 Tokens, says Mr Skeat: see Richtofen, *Friesische Rechtsquellen*, p. 130. Mr Small says that 'no copy of the original is to be found in the Benedictine edition of Jerome's Works'; and Mr Wright states that 'others say they are first found in the *Prognosticon futuri seculi* of Julianus Pomerius, a theologian, who died in the year 690'.)

The Song that follows the *Signs* here, has pretty bits and good words in it.

[*Laud MS*. 622, *leaf* 70, *back, col*. 2.]

¶ ffiftene toknes.   ¶ Ieremie.

St. Jerome's 15 Tokens:

Seint Ieremie telleþ *in* his book ⸝ of xv. tokenyng⸝
 þat god wil a3ein*s* domesdai ⸝ here on erþe bring⸝ :
 þe first day þe Cee schal arise ⸝ & as a wal stonde,
Wel hei3er by .xl feet⸝ ⸝ þan any hil i*n* þis londe.   4

1. The sea rises 40 feet.

þat oþer dai, it schal so lowe ali3t⸝ ⸝ þat vnneþe me*n* schul it se ;

2. it nearly vanishes.

Alle þe fissches þe þrid day ⸝ abouen þe wat*er* schuH be,
& so reuly a c*r*i 3iuen ⸝ þat aH me*n* schullen haue fere ;

3. all fish turn up and cry.

þe fierþe day, wat*er* schal bren*n*e ⸝ as þei3 it coles were ;   8

4. water burns.

þe v^te. day, schal eu*er*ych tre ⸝ blede dropes of blood⸝ ;

5. trees bleed.

þe vj^te. day, schuH castels & houses faH ⸝ aH þat eu*er* stood ;

6. castles fall.

þe vij^te. day, stones schuH fi3tt⸝ ⸝ þe viij . þe erþe q*u*ake ;

7, 8. stones fight, &c.

þe ix^e day, aH hilles sp*re*den abrod ⸝ & al þe werld⸝ euen make ;

9. hills flatten.

þe x. day, me*n* schul ren*n*e aboute ⸝ as þai wode were,   13
As wilde bestes holes to seche ⸝ to hide he*m* i*n*ne for fere.

10. men run like mad, for fear.

// þe xj. day, bones of ded⸝ men ⸝ arise*n* schuH & vpri3t⸝ stonde ;

11. dead bones rise.

þe xij dai, as þei3 it ster*en* weren ⸝ f*r*am heuen to þe londe ; 16

12. stars fall.

þe xiij. dai, vche q*u*ik þing⸝ schal dye ⸝ þe xiiij. fire ali3t⸝,

13. all die.

And bren*n*e al þe middelerd⸝ ⸝ so c*r*ist it wil di3t⸝ ;

14. earth burns.

þe xv. dai, scholle*n* .iiij. Au*n*gels come*n* ⸝ a .iiij. half mydlerde,
& blowen þorou3-out al þe werlde ⸝ þat vche ma*n* schal be aferd⸝ ;

15. four angels shall blow.

ffor i*n* þilk⸝ age he schal arise ⸝ þat god w*a*s in*n*e ded,   21
Of litel more þa*n* .xxx^ti. wy*n*tren ⸝ as ich 3ou habbe ised⸝,

Christ shall arise with his earthly body,

¶ Lamentacio a*n*imar*um*.

[*This is the Head line in the MS, tho' there is no break in the story.*]

[1] Wiþ þilk⸝ body þat he had⸝ here ⸝ he ne schal so litel misse
As þe lest⸝ her of his body ⸝ I sigge 3ou Iwisse. [1 leaf 71] 24

LAMENTACIO ANIMARUM. SONG OF JOY FOR CHRIST'S COMING. 93

Oure lord schal come & smyte adoun ⸭ as liȝttyng doþ to grounde,   *and come down like lightning.*
þere þat he to heuen stiȝe ⸭ with his bledyng wounde.[1]
An Aungel schal þe spere & þe nails ⸭ & þe crovne of þorn,   *An angel shall bear the*
& þe rood þat he died on ⸭ with hym bringe aforn.   28   *spear, nails, cross, &c.*
In þe vale of Iosephat ⸭ his dom he wil do;   *The Doom shall be held*
þe best man schal sore agrise ⸭ þat schal come þerto.   *in the Vale of Jehoshaphat.*
Leuere had his owen moder ⸭ in helle pyne to be,
Al þe while þe dom ylast ⸭ þan her sones face to see.   32
Allas! hou schull we þan ouercome ⸭ þilk griselich fere,
Whan vche seint schal aferde be ⸭ oure lord crist to see þere?

Ovre lord wil schewe his bitter woundes ⸭ And Sigge, "Man!   *Christ will ask who has*
    for þe,   35
    Look what ich haue ysuffred ⸭ what hastow suffred for me?"
Mest he wil vnderstonde þere ⸭ þe vij. merciful dedes :   *done the 7 deeds of*
Who þat haþ hem here ydo ⸭ as he with his mouþ sede,   *Mercy,*
þe hungri forto fede ⸭ & schride þe cloþles,
Ofte goo to sek men ⸭ & herberewe þe housles,   40
þe dede forto bury, ⸭ þe bounden to vnbynde,
þai þat þise on erþe loueden ⸭ þere hij schullen it fynde.   *and reward them.*

Ovre lord wil to þe liþer sigge ⸭ as we reden in gospelle,   *The cursed shall be*
    "Ȝe cursed gostes, goþ ⸭ in-to þe pyne of helle!"   44   *carrid off by devils.*
þe deuelen willen come ȝernend ⸭ & speten fire & blast,
& taken þe wrecched soulen ⸭ & in-to pyne hem cast.

Ovre lord wil to good men sigge ⸭ "in my riȝth honde ȝe come,   *The good, Christ shall*
    And afongeþ my fador riche ⸭ þat aȝeins ȝow is ynome,   *take to his father's*
    þat to ȝou was ymaked ⸭ bifore þe werldes biginnyng;   *kingdom.*
þere ȝe schullen be in ioye with me ⸭ wiþ-outen any endyng."
In þis book we finde ywrite ⸭ þat þre manere folk schal saued be,   *Maiden,*
Maidenhod & spousehod ⸭ & widewehode : þise þre.   52   *spouse, and widow, shall*
Ich bid hym þat vs deme schal ⸭ kyng of all kynge,   *be sav'd.*
Among his blissed sones ⸭ oure soules to heuen brynge. Amen.

Off ioye & blisse is my song ⸭ care to bileue,   *A Song of Joy that that*
    & to herie hym among ⸭ þat al oure soroȝ schal reue.   4   *honey-drop, Christ, has*
    Ycome he is, þat swete dew ⸭ þat swete hony drope,   *come.*

[1] MS. woudē

	Iesus, kynge of alle kynges ꞉ to whom is al oure hope.	8
	Bicome he is oure broþer ꞉ whare was he so longe ;	
He bought us. We may call him Brother.	He it is, & non oþer ꞉ þat bouȝth vs so stronge.	12
	Oure broþer we mowe hym clepe wel ꞉ so seiþ hym-self ilome,	
	& so ne miȝtten þai neuer adel ꞉ þat bifore vs come.	16
He took our flesh, to make us one with him.	He nas oure broþer nouȝth ꞉ er he oure flesch nome ;	
	þerwiþ he haþ vs dere abouȝth ꞉ to maken vs ysome.	20
	ysome nere we nouȝth bifore ꞉ Aungels & oure kynde,	
	Er swete Iesus were ybore ꞉ þat to selde is in mynde.	24
	// Bot now he haþ oure flesch ynome ꞉ & oure broþer is ;	
	Oure kynde is wel heiȝe ycome ꞉ among oþer, Iwis ;	28
	ffor he is oure kynde heixt ꞉ saue his godhede,	
	& al aboue his throne next ꞉ so heiȝe is manhede.	32
Angels are not so near him as we are.	Aungel ne worþ hym nouȝt so neiȝ ꞉ for he is oure broþer nouȝth,	
	& þat oure kynde is ek so heiȝe ꞉ he haþ vs dere abouȝth.	36
	Aungels he ne bouȝth nouȝth ꞉ we ben hym wel neer ;	
	Whan he haþ vs so dere bouȝth ꞉ wel ouȝtten we to louen hym here.	40
Angels are only his messengers, and they shall serve us in heaven.	Ne aungel nys naþemo ꞉ bot his messagere, [leaf 71, col. 2]	
	How miȝth it þan go ꞉ to be his broþer here ?	44
	& in heuen þai schullen also ꞉ whan þat we ben þere,	
	Oure hestes & oure will do ꞉ as þai oure hynen were,	48
	And to oure heste seruen vs ꞉ to foot & to honde,	
	Oure owen mowe we holden hem ꞉ as ich vnderstonde ;	52
	wel mowe we þan glade be ꞉ to habbe suich an hyne.	
	& siþþe we mowe here isee ꞉ as we iseþ atte fyne,	56
We are highest of all, except God.	þat we ben alþer kynde heiȝest ꞉ wiþ-oute god al-one,	
	And in heuen also hym next ꞉ among his aungels vchone.	60
	And all þat now late comen ꞉ siþ oure lorde aliȝth,	
Blessed be his might !	And oure flesch haþ here ynomen ꞉ yheried be his miȝth !	64
	þilk þat toforne vs come ꞉ whan þai þe deþ founde,	
Before us, all men went to hell.	þan were þai onon ycast ꞉ in-to helle grounde.	68
	Nere he neuer so holy ne so good ꞉ þere nas non forbore ;	
	And so hem longed sore ꞉ after oure lorde þerfore.	72

A SONG OF JOY FOR CHRIST'S COMING.

// þe prophetes þat weren so good ꞉ & so holy alle, *The prophets*
þat of oure lorde vnderstoden ꞉ & what schulde bi-fall, 76
Hij wisten þat he schulde come ꞉ ac hij nysten whanne; 78
þe tyme hem þouȝt long ynouȝ ꞉ vche ynche hem þouȝt a spanne. *thought it long ere Christ came.*
þai gradden after hym oft ꞉ in her prophecie, 82
And in þe bokes þat þai writen ꞉ þat he schulde dye: 84
"God ȝeue," quoþ on of hem ꞉ "þat heuen broste atwo, *One prayd that heaven might burst, and Christ alight to save men.*
þat he miȝth aliȝth adoun ꞉ & vs sauen so." 88
Sumdel hem longed þo ꞉ whan þai nolden abide,
þat heuen cleue soft a two ꞉ to saue vche side. 92 *But tho' they wisht the heaven to cleave,*
Ac it schulde al to brest ꞉ & oure lorde falle adoune,
Miȝth þai hym haue yhent ꞉ fast by þe crovne. 96
Ac he ne heiȝed nouȝth so swiþ ꞉ bot com soft adoun; 98
þai wolde hym narewȝ hab y-hent ꞉ ac he held hem þer doun.
Parde, ȝit ne com he nouȝth ꞉ ne were hem neuer so wo; 102 *Christ came not to them.*
þai hadden þe grounde of helle isouȝth ꞉ er he com hem to. 104
Seint Dauid after his anoie ꞉ after hym grad þus: *David cried after Him,*
"Lord, in heuen to vs abowȝe ꞉ & aliȝth to vs! 108
Schewe vs þine holy face ꞉ & we worþe hool onon."
Hym longed ek after his face ꞉ þe holy Symeon, 112 *and so did holy Simeon.*
And all blis hym was bynome ꞉ & oft he gradd þerfore:
"Lorde, whan wiltou come ꞉ & wilt ben ybore? 116
Wene ȝe ich may dure ꞉ wene ȝe ich may see?"
Her mone was doel to see ꞉ þere gamed hem no gle. 120
// Ac hym ne greued nouȝth ꞉ aȝeins oþer bifore,
ffor he nas nouȝth to deþ ibrouȝth ꞉ er god were ibore, 124
Ac liued forto he hym seiȝ ꞉ & in his armes nome, *And Simeon livd to take Christ in his arms.*
þo he on Candelmesday ꞉ to þe temple come. 128
Lorde, wel may vs be ꞉ bet þan hem was þo, *How well for us*
þat ne miȝtten nower fle ꞉ lorde, what hem was wo. 132
þere oure lorde seide ꞉ þo he was ybore,
þat we miȝtten ben ful glade ꞉ ouer oþer þat weren bifore. 136 *that we can see Him whom Prophets and Kings longd in vain to see; and that we may gain heaven for nought,*
þe prophetes wilned hym forto see ꞉ & many kynges also,
þat we isen ȝif it miȝth be ꞉ ac hij ne miȝtten it nouȝth do.
// we mowen now as it were ꞉ for nouȝth, to heuen come, 142
Siþþen oure lord it had ibouȝth ꞉ & þe fendes power bynome.

since Christ has bought it for us!	Ac þai þat suich grace ne hadden ⸭ þat tofore vs come,	146
	After oure lorde þai gradden ⸭ in þe prophecie ylome;	148
	After hym þai gradden ⸭ wiþ greť wille & longe;	
	No mendementˊ þai ne seie ⸭ boť greť pyne & stronge;	152
They longd for Him till they were weary,	So longe þat þai wery weren ⸭ & leten be al stille,	
	And he[r] gredyngˊ forberen ⸭ & turneden to goddes wille;	156
	ffor þai ne seizen non oþer won ⸭ þouȝ hem þouȝtten longe;	
	Oure lorde lete her will ago ⸭ er he wolde flesch a-fonge.	160
	And þo þai weren wery ynouȝ ⸭ as who seiþ for sore,	
	Vche of hem to restˊ drouȝ ⸭ & speken of hym nomore,	164
and then that sweet bairn took our nature, to fell the fiend. God grant us a place in heaven!	þat swete barne oure kynde tookˊ ⸭ boþe of flesche & felle,	
	In whiche he dyed on roodˊ ⸭ þe fendes strengþe to felle.	168
	Þorouȝ whiche preciouse deþ ⸭ god vs grant þat grace	
	þat we mowe after oure deþ ⸭ in heuen haue a place. Amen.	172

SOLOMON'S CORONATION, DEEDS, AND JUDGMENT ON THE TWO MOTHERS' CLAIM TO ONE CHILD. HIS COURT AND TEMPLE.

[In order to complete the Life of Solomon, of which his *Book of Wisdom*, &c., form part, I add the MS. bit that comes before the *Book*. The passage about his birth is too far back to be taken.]

[*Laud MS.* 622, *leaf* 69, *col.* 1.]

Adonijah tries to be king in David's lifetime (1 *Kings* i. 5—10).	¶ Þo Dauid in elde was ⸭ his eldest son was alyue.	
	Adonye ycleped he was ⸭ with Salamon he gan striue.	
	Aboute he was kyngˊ to be ⸭ by his fader daye.	
	Gretˊ feste he made on a day ⸭ þat folkˊ to paye.	4*
	He ne badˊ nowgth þider Salamon ⸭ ne his moder þe quene;	
	þerfore sche was with hym wroþ ⸭ for wymmen beþ oftˊ kene.	
But Bathsheba appeals to David on Solomon's behalf (1 *Kings* i. 15—21).	"Sir," sche seide to Dauid ⸭ "oftˊ þou swore me,	
	þat my son Salamon ⸭ schulde be kyngˊ after þe.	8*
	Now haþ Adonye iþouȝth to be kyngˊ bi þi lyue;	
	& after þi day to sle my son ⸭ for þai ne ben by on wyue."	

SOLOMON'S CORONATION, MARRIAGE, AND JUDGMENT.

Þ E kyng˙ lete somony aH his men : a fest˙ he made sone, [col. 2]
 And lete coroone Salamon ; & sette hym in his throne.
 By his lyue he made hym kyng ; & bigan to prechi fast˙
ffor to sustene vp goddes lawȝe ; þer-while his lif ylast˙ ;
þat he bulde forþ goddes hous in Ierusalems burghȝ,
þat þe lawȝes better weren ; ysustened þorouȝ & þorouȝ.   16*
Dauid was kyng˙ fourty wyntren ; in werre & in strife ;
And in þe fourtide ȝer ; in pes he ended his lyf˙.

A ffter e his fader, Salamon ; slouȝ his broþer Adonye
 In þe first ȝer, & aH þat with hym weren ; to hym he
  made boweye,   20*
& he wex faiþful man & wis ; þat folk˙ better to wisse,
þe kynges douȝttere of Egipte ; he wedded in gret blisse.
þe grete þinges forto don ; he destred¹ goddes grace,
ffor to arere goddes temple ; in on faire place,   24*
And aboute Ierusalem ; treble wal arere.
þat to his bihofþe & vche riche kyng˙ ; þe court arered were,
His sacrifise he dude to god ; & gan to hym crie :
" Lorde ! " he seide, " to ȝong icham ; to haue suich maistrie.
Teche me, ȝif þi wille be ; wel my folk˙ to wisse,   29*
And to knowe god˙ & yuel ; þat I þerof ne mysse."
Oure lord˙ hym graunted þinges þre ; to haue maistri ouer
 his fo,
To habbe worldes richesse ynouȝ ; & wisdom ynouȝ þerto.

I T bifel þat two wymmen ; in on In, a niȝth were ;   33*
 Eiþer had˙ a ȝong˙ childe ; boþe of on ȝere.
 In hire slep þat o womman ; her owen childe ouerlay,
And siþþe leide it by her felawe ; & hir child˙ nom away.   36*
Þo þe womman awook˙ ; & vnderȝat˙ þis gile,
Ȝerne þai striueden & chid˙ · for þe quik˙ child˙ a long˙ while.
þat on seide, þe quyk˙ childe was hire ; þat oþer seide it nas.
Boþe þei comen bifore þe kyng˙ ; & tolden al her cas.   40*
¶ Þo þe kyng˙ ne miȝth vnderȝete ; wheþer had þe riȝth,
" Take hider," he seide, " my swerd˙ ; & euen, I wil it diȝth ;
Cleuen ich wil, ȝif ich can ; þe quyk˙ childe a two.
& taken eiþer of ȝou þe haluendel ; whan ȝe nyllen oþer do."

ADAM DAVY   7

Marginalia:

David has Solomon crowned (1 Kings i. 32—40),

and dies in the 40th year of his reign (1 Kings ii. 10, 11).

Solomon slays Adonijah (1 Kings ii. 24-5),

weds the king of Egypt's daughter (1 Kings iii. 1),

[¹ ? desired]

and prays to God for wisdom (1 Kings iii. 6—9;.

(1 Kings iii. 16—28.)

A woman who had overlaid her child, put it by another mother, and took her living babe away.

They strove, and came before Solomon.

He ordered the living babe to be cut in halves.

The false mother agreed;	"ȝe, sir," seide þe fals quene ! "crist' it' ȝelde þe ;	45*
	So þou miȝth best legge strif ! þan mowe we euen be."	
the true one gave up her child.	"Nay, sir," seide þe riȝth moder ! "mercy, þat do þou nouȝth !	
	Take hire raþer euerich del ! þat it ne be to deþ ybrouȝth."	
To her, Solomon adjudgd the babe.	"ȝe, good womman," þe kyng' seide ! "take þat child' to þe ;	
	ffor þou hast' þe riȝth weye ! & þe oþere þe falste."	

Folk wonderd at his wisdom.

Michel wonder hadden al þat folk' · þat herden of þis strif',
þat þe kyng' þouȝth swich wisdom ! in his ȝong' lyf'. 52*
Men douteden þerafter-ward hym þe more ! for þilk cas.
Good pais þere was in hil londe ! þer while he kyng' was.

The weekly food for Solomon's household (1 Kings iv. 22-3).	Vche weke he spended in his hous ! xxx. quarters of whete,	
	And an hundreþ fatte weþers ! & xxx. Oxen grete,	56*
	Wiþouten venison & oþer þing' ! þat he had' by deinte :	
	In þe werlde was non so riche court' ! ne of so gret plente.	
His triple wall round Jerusalem.	He arered treble wal ! swiþe fair & strong'	
	Aboute þe burghȝ of Ierusalem ! swiþe fair & long'.	60*
His Temple.	þe fierþe ȝer of his regne ! he gan his temple arere,	
	& in þe elleuenþe ȝer was it ! er it redy were.	
His Court.	þo bigan he arere his court' ! swiþe noble & hende ;	
	Xiij. ȝer þer-aboute he was ! er it were brouȝth to ende.	64*

[*For what follows, see p.* 82, *above.* The Book of Wisdom may be compard with the A B C, and How the Good Wife and Good Man taught their Daughter and Son, in my *Babees Book*, *Q. Elizabethes Achademy*, &c., and with Mr Lumby's *Ratis Raving*, &c, &c.]

NOTES.

p. 17. The version of *Alexius* in Barbour's great collection of Saints' Lives in the unique MS. Gg. 2. 6, in the University Library, Cambridge, I leave for Mr Bradshaw's long-projected edition of that book. The Durham version, Canon Greenwell kindly tells me, " agrees in the main with Laud MS. 108 and Vernon MS. (p. 20 above), as you will see from the part I have transcribed. The Life is contained in a MS. V. ii. 14, fol. 92 recto, Cosin's Library, together with The destruction of Thebes, Cato in verse (St Alexius), Life of St Margaret, Life of St Mary Magdalene in prose. It is written not-verse fashion."

Uita Sancti Alexi Confessoris

Sitteth stille with outen stryf.
And j wille tellen yow of the lyf.
Of an holy man ⸵   3
Alexywys was his name.
to serue god thoght him no shame.
therof neu*ere* he ne blan.   6

¶ His fader was a gret lordyng.
Of rome a kynges euenyng.
And hight Eufemyan ⸵   9
Pore men to clothe and feede.
In al rome that ryche stede.
Suche ne was ther nan.   12

¶ Eu*ere*che day weren in his halle.
Yleyde thre bordes for to calle.
Pore men forto feede ⸵   15
Hem to serue he was ful glade.
He did as Ihu crist hym bade.
He hopede therfore to haue his meete.   18

¶ Whan thei weren serued by and by.
Than was he redy.
to gone to his mete ⸵   21
ffor the loue of godes sone.
With men of relygyōne
Wolde he sytte and ete.   24

  ¶ Hys wyf hight dame Aglaes.
  To sey the sothe with outen les.
  that moche was to preyse !   27
  But she did the same maner.
  As dyd hir lord as ye myght here.
  she was noght at ese.   30
  ¶ Children by twene hem hadde thei none.
  Therof to god thei made her mone.
  bothe day and nyght !   33
  Iħu cryst he herde her bone.
  And sent hem a ful goode sone.
  her hertes for to lyght.   36
  ¶ Sone as he was borne that blessyd childe.
  Alix bothe meke and mylde.
  And of maneres hende !   39
  Sone after with gret haste.
  Thei avowed bothe hem chaste.
  to her lyues ende.   42

 Prof. Schipper of Vienna has just publisht a critical edition of what he considers the oldest English version of the Alexius, that from the Vernon and Laud 108 (p. 20 above), with collations from the Naples quarto MS., formerly O. 4 n 6—12, A. 47, later XIII. B. 29 (A.D. 1457), of which Mr David Laing gave the following specimen in *Reliquiæ Antiquæ* (1843), ii. 64-5 :—

 P. 80—86. Of Seint Alex of Rome

   Sitteth still withouten [s]trife
   Ycche wolle you telle the life
   Of an holi man :
   Alex was his right[e] name ;
   To servy God he thouȝt no schame,
   Ther of never he ne blan

   His father was a grete lordlyng,
   Of Rome a kyng[es] evenyng,
   And hight Sur Eufamyan :
   Pore men to clothe and fede,
   In al Rom, that riche stede,
   Suche ne was ther nan.
    Explicit vita Sancti Alex.

In all, 618 lines, or 103 stanzas of six lines each.

 p. 89, l. 245. *Abacuc and his top.* The Apocrypha version of this story (*Bel and the Dragon*, verse 33-4) makes Habbacuc a prophet in Jury; and says, that after Daniel had eaten his pottage and bread, "the angel of the Lord set Habbacuc in his own place again immediately."

INDEX OF WORDS AND SUBJECTS,

MAINLY BY

MR. SIDNEY J. HERRTAGE, B.A., TRIN. COLL., DUBLIN.

In the *St. Alexius* references, L. i. stands for Laud MS. 622; L. ii. for Laud 108; L. iii. for Laud 463. C. is for Cotton, Titus, A xxvi; V. for the Vernon MS.; and T. for the Trinity (Oxford) 57. 20/57 means page 20, line 57.

A, L. 20/57, up; awook, awoke.
Abod, V. 68/464, *v. pt. t.* endurd, livd until. A.S. *abidan*.
Abouȝe, 82/28, *v.* bow down. A.S. *abogan*.
Abouȝth, 94/20, *pp.* bought, redeemed. A.S. *abycgan*.
Ac, L. iii. 27/107; T. 27/107, *conj.* but.
Acesse, L. i. 68/1041, *v.* stop, put an end to, make to cease.
Acursy, 86/142, *v.* curse.
Adel, 94/16, *adv.* a bit, in the least, at, all.
Adradd, 86/161, *pp.* afraid, frightend.
A-Feryd, C. 58/282, *pp.* afraid.
Affter, C. 47/227, *prep.* according to; affter me, according to my will.
Affye, L. i. 27/178, *v.* trust. Fr. *affier*.
Afliȝth, L. i. 62/948, *pp.* afflicted, uneasy, disturbd.
Afong, L. iii. 24/44; Vnderfonge, T. 24/44, *v.* take, receive. O. L. Ger. *fangan*; afongeþ, 93/48, *imper.* receive.
Aforn, 93/28, *prep.* in front, before.
Agast, L. i. 27/170, *adj.* astonisht, afraid.
Agloes (mother of St. Alexius), 22; her lamentation over her son, 68.
Agrise, 93/30, *v.* be afraid; agros, L. iii. 29/143; T. 29/143, *v. pt. t.* was frightend, trembld. A.S. *agrisan*.

Ak, L. i. 47/588, *conj.* but.
Akneo, L. iii. 57/384, *adv.* on their knees.
Alegge, 85/113, *v.* lighten, ease. A.S. *alecgan*. See Wedgwood, *s.* allege.
Alesed, L. i. 49/651, *pp.* praisd, renownd.
ALEXIUS, St., his family, 20, 21; his birth and christening, 24; his education, 25; his father chooses him a wife, 26; he is marrid, 27; takes farewell of his wife, 29; starts off on a pilgrimage, 31; arrives at Galys, 32; goes to Syria, 33; gives away all his clothes and money, 34; his friends send to seek for him, 35; the messengers do not know him, 39; is pointed out by the image of the Virgin, 42; is honourd by the Syrians, 44; flees to Galicia, 45; sets sail to Tarsus, but is driven to Rome, 46; asks his father for alms, 49; is receivd into his father's house, 51; ill-treated by his father's servants, 53; writes his life, 54; a voice from heaven speaks about him, 57; his death is foretold, 58; his death, 59; his father questiond about him, 60; he will not give up his book to the Emperor, 63; gives it up to the Pope, 64; his life read to the pecple, 65; burid at the

Church of St. Boniface, 74; miracles workt by his corpse, 75.

Aleye, C. 26/64, *s.* friend, alliance.

Alite, *s.* 88/225, a little.

Aliȝt, 90/295, *adj.* burning, flaming.

Aliȝt, 92/5, *v.* settle down, sink. A.S. *alihtan.*

Aliȝth, 87/199, *v. pt. t.* came down. A.S. *alihtan.*

Almesse, L. ii. 33/99; Almus, V. 33/99, *s.* alms. A.S. *ælmesse.*

Almest, L. iii. 74/562, *adv.* almost, nearly.

Alonged, 87/185, *pp.* longing, anxious.

Alre, V. 41/186; Alþres, L. ii. 41/186; Alþer, 94/57, *gen. pl.* of all.

Amended, 84/65, *pp.* assisted, benefited.

Among, 93/4 (in the Song), *adv.* constantly? (generally 'at intervals.')

Amongus, V. 33/100, *prep.* amongst.

Amorwe, T. 42/271, *adv.* in the morning.

Anan, L. i. 60/391, *adv.* presently.

Aniȝth, L. i. 24/129, *adv.* in the night, at night.

Ankre, L. i. 39/420, *s.* anchorite.

Annys, The city of, 33; The image of the Virgin at, 34.

Anoie, 95/105, *s.* trouble.

Antichrist, p. 89, 90; shall go only into the Holy Land, 89/271; shall turn many to evil, 90/285; shall slay Enoch and Elijah, and be killd by the Holy Ghost, 90/289—296.

Apertely, L. i. 55/776, *adv.* plainly.

Apliȝth, L. i. 48/613, *adv.* completely, quite.

Aquited, L. i. 31/248, *v. pt. t.* paid.

Archadius and Honorius, the Emperors of Rome, enquire about Alexius, p. 60; try to get Alexius's book from his corpse, 62.

Are, V. 32/84, *adv.* before, ere.

Arere, 97/22, *v.* rear, raise, build. A.S. *arœran.*

Arne, C. 68/356, *v. pr. t.* are.

Asaye, C. 66/337, *v.* attempt.

A-slawe, T. 31/165; Y-slawe, L. iii. 31/165, *pp.* slain.

Astond, L. iii. 37/234; Astonde, T. 37/234, *pp.* upstood, landed, settled; Astonde, L. iii. 45/288; T. iii. 45/288, *v. inf.* land.

Aswoȝe, T. 29/141; Yswowe, L. iii. 29/141, *adj.* in a swoon, fainting. A.S. *swogan.*

At Arst, L. ii. 22/20; first. Aterst= indeed.—Cole's Dict.

Atayse, L. ii. 23/30, at ease.

Atende, L. iii. 64/441, *vb. pt. t.* lighted up; *tenden,* to kindle, light, burn.

Atom, V. 36/122, *adv.* at home.

Atterliche, L. iii. 29/143, *adv.* bitterly.

Aȝe, T. 26/88; Aȝein, L. iii. 26/88, *adv.* again, back.

Autere, 15/139, *s.* altar.

Auȝte, L. iii. 72/545; Oȝte, T. 72/545, *v. pt. t.* ought.

Auȝtte, L. i. 30/228, *s.* possession.

Auenture, L. i. 73/1085, *s.* fortune.

Avoweden, L. i. 24/122; Auouwede, L. ii. 24/41; V. 24/41, *v. pt. t.* vowd. Fr. *avouer.*

Awey, T. 73/547, *interj.* alas.

Awreke, 14/104, avengd. A.S. *wrecan.*

Axen, L. i. 36/362, *v.* enquire, hear of.

Axste, T. 68/491, *v. pt. t.* askt.

Ayre, C. 38/148, *s.* hair cloth.

Ayþer, L. i. 26/157, one, each.

Aȝeins, L. i. 21/73, *adv.* against.

Aȝeins, 92/2, *prep.* before; 93/48, for, in readiness for. A.S. *ongean.*

Aȝeinward, 12/19, *adv.* back, in return.

Bachelers, L. 121/80, *s. pl.* young warriors, squires. Lat. *baccalaureus.*

Bad, L. ii. 48/297, *v. pt. t.* beggd.

Bale, L. iii. 29/140, *s.* sorrow, trouble.

Barayne, L. i. 22/97, *adj.* childless. O. Fr. *baraigne.*

Baret, 83/34, *s.* quarrel, contest. O. Fr. *barat.*

Barme, L². 34/300, *s.* breast, bosom. A.S. *bearm.*

INDEX OF WORDS AND SUBJECTS. 103

Barne, 96/165, *s.* child. Scot. *bairn.*
Bede, L. iii. 23/28; T. 23/28, *v. pt. t.*, beggd, prayd. A.S. *bidan.*
Bede, 14/118, *v. pt. t.* bade. A.S. *beodan.*
Bedeman, L. i. 49/658, *s.* beadsman, one who offerd up prayers for the welfare of another.
Bedene, C. 77/415, *adv.* at once, completely.
Bedeyes, C. 41/186, *s. pl.* prayers, beads.
Beere, V. 74/557; Bere, L. i. 74/1096, *s.* bier.
Beie, *adj.* 87/174, both.
Belde, V. 26/49; L. ii. 26/49, *v.* increase in size and strength, to furnish out; cf. our 'man of large build.'
Bellewarde, L. iii. 41/267; Belward, T. 41/267, bell-ringer.
Bem, T. 64/440; Beom, L. iii. 64/440, *s.* beam.
Berd, L. iii. 51/318, *s.* beard.
Bere, L. iii. 29/129, *s.* voice, words. A.S. (ge)*bære.*
Beryng 15/135, *s.* birthday, nativity.
Beshoppys, C. 26/62, *s. pl.* bishops. A.S. *biscop,* from Lat. *episcopus.*
Besshope, C. 60/289, *s.* bishop.
Bete, L. iii. 29/135; T. 29/135, *v.* amend, abate, atone for. A.S. *betan.*
Beteche, L. iii. 31/178; Byteche, *v. pr. t.* betake to, commit to.
Betyght, L. iii. 76/596, *pp.* deckt, envelopt. A.S. *bityhtan.*
Beyȝ, L. iii. 63/433; Beiȝ, T. 63/433, *v. pt. t.* bowd. A.S. *began.*
Bi, 96/9, *prep.* bi þi lyue = during thy life, whilst thou art alive.
Bid, 93/53, *v. pr. t.* pray.
Biddeth, 14/112, *v. imp.* pray, offer. A.S. *bidden.*
Bien, 14/104, *v.* to be. A.S. *beon.*
Bifalle, 16/154, *v.* happen, come to pass.
Bigile, L. i. 47/589 *v.* deceive, cheat.

Bihofþe, 97/28, *s.* benefit.
Bihynde, 83/31, *adv.* behind, hanging back, and so false.
Bilaue, L. i. 19/21; Bileue, 83/62, *v.* cease, leave off.
Bileue, 14/100, *v.* remain, stay. A.S. *bilæfan.*
Bileue, 88/231, *s.* belief, religion.
Bileued, L. i. 35/325, *pp.* left, remaining.
Birth of St. Alexius, 24.
Bisouȝth, L. i. 32/262, *v. pt. t.* besought.
Bitake, L. i. 23/113, *v.* give, bequeath. See *Beteche* above.
Bitauȝtte, L. i. 33/286, *v. pt. t.* betook, committed to, commended.
Biþouȝten, L. i. 76/1117, *v. pt. t.* bethought, thought. A.S. *bithincan.*
Bitook, 15/137, *v. pt. t.* took. A.S. *bitacan.*
Bitraye, 83/62, *v.* betray.
Blan, L. ii. 20/6; Blon, V. 20/6, *v. pt. t.* ceast. A.S. *blinnan.*
Blast, 93/45, *s.* wind.
Blede, L. iii. 22/27; T. 22/27, *s.* lit. blood, hence family, children.
Blee, 15/140, *s.* colour.
Bleyss, C. 71/370, *s.* bliss, heaven.
Blin, V. 60/389; Blyn, L. ii. 60/389, *v.* stop.
Blissed, 88/217, *v. pt. t.* blessed.
Blynne, L. i. 35/348, *v.* cease.
Bo, L. iii. 38/235, *adj.* both.
Boke, L. i. 25/133, *s.* learning, school.
Bon, 83/38, *s.* bone.
Bone, 12/49, *s.* prayer, request. O. Icel. *bón.*
Boniface, St. Alexius married at the Church of, 27. St. Alexius buried at, 74.
Boost, L. i. 64/975, *s.* noise, disturbance.
Borde, 83/31, *s.* table. A.S. *bord,* Goth. *baurd.* "Boorde, *tabula, mensa.*"—Prompt. Parv.
Bordes, L. ii. 21/14; Bordus, V. 21/14, *s. pl.* tables.

Bore, 12/46, *pp.* born.
Boredes, C. 22/15, tables. A.S. *bord.*
Borgh, T. 32/181 : Bour, L. iii. 32/181 ; Burhg, L. iii. 21/13, *s.* town. A.S. *burg, burh.*
Bote, L. ii. 23/28 ; But, V. 23/28, *conj.* unless, except.
Bote, L. i. 75/1109, *s.* help, relief.
Boþome, 84/81, *s.* bottom.
Boun, V. 38/136, *adj.* ready, prepared.
Boure, L. i. 60/888, *s.* chamber.
Boweye, 97/20, *v.* bow down, become subject.
Bowȝe, 84/71, *v.* bow to, give way to.
Brak, L. iii. 29/127 ; *v. pt. t.* brake ; he broke off. Brake, T. 29/127, it broke up. (?)
Brede, T. 29/128, bride.
Breech, L. i. 53/731, *s.* breeches.
Brennyng, 86/164, *v. pr. t.* burning.
Breyde, L. i. 37/396, *v. pt. t.* to breyde = pulld asunder (? not tore in pieces).
Broht, L. iii. 52/329, *s.* See Broþ.
Broste, 95/86, *v.* burst. A.S. *berstan.*
Broþ, V. 52/310, *s.* Broþ of fissches, water in which fishes had been boiled.
Bryght, C. 29/88, *s.* bright one, (?) bride.
Bulde, 97/14, *v.* build. A.S. *byldan.*
Burghȝ, 97/14, *s.* city.
Buste, L. iii. 53/331, *v. pt. t.* burst, broke his skin, or bustled, hustled, (burst, T.).
By, 84/70, *prep.* against.
By, 96/3, *adv.* before.
By, 97/6 ; L. i. 73/1090, *prep.* during, in ; by his lyue = during his lifetime.
By, L. i. 37/381, *v.* be. A.S. *beon.*
Byffell, C. 20/4, *v. pt. t.* happend.
Bynome, 95/143, *pp.* taken away.
Bysmare, L. i. 71/1064, *s.* disgrace, outrage.
Byt, C. 27/70, *conj.* but.
By-wake, T. 76/600, *v.* watch by.
Bywent, L. i. 27/171, *v. pt. t.* became.

Candelmesday, 95/128, *s.* Candlemas Day, Feb. 2, the Purification of the so-calld Virgin Mary.
Catel, L. i. 46/575, *s.* goods, property, chattels. O. Fr. *catel,* Lat. *capitale.*
Cee, L. i. 31/244, *s.* the sea.
Celli, V. 34/104, *s.* (selly L. ii.) blessed object, relic. A.S. *sælig beatus.*
Cenatoure, L. i. 20/65, *s.* a senator.
Cette, C. 26/58, *s.* city.
Chalenged, L. i. 60/880, *v. pt. t.* questiond, chargd.
Chanse, they leuyd, C. 24/36, (?) a miswriting for ' chaste they livede.'
Chapman, L. ii. 32/82, *s.* merchant. A.S. *ceapman.*
Chaunceler, L. i. 64/968, *s.* chancellor.
Chere, 11/12, *s.* countenance.
Cheryte, C. 41/182, *s.* charity, alms.
Ches, 15/148, *v. pt. t.* chose. A.S. *ceosian.*
Cheste, V. 61/401, *s.* strife, quarrelling.
Chide, 83/51, *v. imper.* argue, quarrel.
Chircheward, L. i. 32/258, *adv.* towards the church.
Ciclatounes, L. i. 38/397, *s. pl.* a sort of cloak, made of siclatoun or siglaton, a rich kind of stuff brought from the East. See Halliwell, *s. v.* Cyclas.
Clepe, 94/13, *v.* call. A.S. *cleopian.*
Cleped, L. iii. 20/8; Y-clepud, T. 20/8, *pp.* named, calld. A.S. *cleopian.*
Clers, L. i. 21/79, *adj.* bright, shining.
Clethe, C. 50/244, *s.* clothes.
Cleue, 95/92, *v.* cleave, open.
Cloop, L. i. 61/923, *s.* clothing.
Cloþles, 93/39, *adj.* naked.
Clyppe, L. i. 68/1044, *v.* embrace, clasp.
Colde, L. i. 37/380, coldness, want of heat of youth.
Con, V. 32/84, *v. pt. t.* knew. A.S. *cunnan.*
Conseile, L. i. 27/168, *s.* council, councillors.
Conuey, 14/101, *v.* conduct, guide.

Coppe, C. 27/75, *s.* cup.
Corage, 87/194, *s.* spirit.
Corce, C. 76/400, *s.* corpse.
Coronation of Solomon, 97.
Coroone, 97/2, *v.* crown ; lete coroone = causd to be crownd.
Cors, V. 63/420 ; Corps, L. ii. 63/420, *s.* corpse, body. Fr. *cors*, Lat. *corpus*.
Couþe, 82/1, *v. pt. t.* knew, understood. A.S. *cunnan*, pt. t. *ic cuðe*.
Cristendom, L. iii. 24/44 ; T. 24/44, *s.* baptism.
Cristenmesse, 13/70, *s.* Christmas.
Cristiente, 12/48 ; Cristianete, 13/82, *s.* Christendom.
Croice, L. i. 59/866, *s.* the cross.
Crokede, L. iii. 75/578, *adj.* deformed, lame.
Crommes, L. i. 50/661, *s. pl.* crumbs.
Croun, V. 52/312, *s.* head.
Cuntrees, L. i. 35/346, *s. pl.* countries.
Curteis, L. i. 21/81, *adj.* courteous.
Custe, V. 70/501, *v. pt. t.* kisst.
Custyume, C. 22/14, *s.* custom, habit.
Cyte, C. 20/4, *s.* city.

Daniel in the lions' den, 89 ; fed by Habbacuc, 89.
DAVY, Adam, Marshal of Stratford-at-Bow, 14/113, 15/149, 16/163.
Dawe, 88/235, *s.* day, life. Bringe of dawe = deprive of life.
Daye, 96/3, *v. pt. t.* died.
Dde, C. 73/385, *v.* die.
Deciples, 89/272, *s. pl.* disciples, followers.
Decollacioun, 12/37, *s.* beheading. Lat. *collum* = the neck.
Ded, C. 66/339, *v. pt. t.* didst.
Def, L. i. 34/293, *adj.* deaf. A.S. *deaf*.
Del, V. 66/450, *s.* a pity. A.S. *deol* = grief.
Dele, 83/61, *v. imper.* distribute.
Delful, V. 66/449, *adj.* doleful, pitiable.

Delite, 84/63, *v. imper.* delight, be pleasd.
Delte, L. iii. 33/197, *v. pt. t.* divided. A.S. *dælan*.
Dent, L. i. 25/143, *s.* blow, stroke. A.S. *dynt*.
Deope, L. iii. 32/190 ; Dep, T. 32/190, *adj.* deep.
Deore, L. iii. 79/632 ; Dere, T. 79/632, *adv.* dearly.
Departed, 86/138, *pp.* divided.
Dere, 94/20, *adv.* dearly. A.S. *deore*.
Derk, 15/121, *s.* darkness. A.S. *dearc*, *deorc*.
Derkhede, 89/269, *s.* darkness.
Derworþ, 12/50, *adj.* dear, precious. A.S. *deorwyrðe*.
Despens, L. i. 31/248, *s.* expenses.
Dethe, C. 77/410, deaf. Cf. *afirst*, for 'athirst,' &c.
Dette, 88/224, *s.* debt. Fr. *debte*, Lat. *debitum*.
Deye, L. i. 60/892, *v.* die.
Dien, L. iii. 71/533, *v.* die.
Digne, L. i. 34/299, *adj.* noble, worthy. Lat. *dignus*.
Diȝe, 87/192, *v.* die.
Diȝth, L. i. 19/28, *v.* prepare. A.S. *dihtan*.
Diȝth, L. i. 37/382, *pp.* set, fixt.
Dissches, V. 52/311, *s. pl.* dishes.
Doȝty, T. 20/7 ; Doughty, L. iii. 20/7, *adj.* valiant, noble. A.S. *dohtig*.
Doloure, L. i. 44/513, *s.* grief, lamentation. O. Fr. *dolur*, *doleur*, Lat. *dolor*.
Dome, C. 77/410, *adj.* dumb.
Domesdai, 92/2, *s.* the day of judgment.
Don, 14/94, *pp.* put to death.
Doom, the Day of ; its signs ; 89/265 ; p. 92, 93.
Doomsday ; St. Jerome's 15 tokens before it, p. 92.
Dooþ, 16/154, *v. imp.* put, place, cause to be put.

Douȝtter, L. i. 26/154, *s.* daughter. A.S. *dohtor.*
Douȝttiest, L. i. 25/143, *adj.* mightiest. A.S. *dohtig.*
Doute, L. iii. 25/71, *s.* trouble, danger.
Douteden, 98/53,- *v. pt. t.* feard, revered.
Douten, 82/13, *v.* fear.
Douttren, 83/42, *s. pl.* daughters.
Drem, T. 68/487, *s.* noise. A.S. *dream.*
Dreri, V. 38/133, *adj.* sad, dreary.
Dreued, L. i. 35/326, *pp.* driven; todreued=driven apart. A.S. *drifan.*
Drey, L. iii. 53/337, *v. pt. t.* went through, sufferd. A.S. *dreogan.*
Dright, L. iii. 23/35; Dryȝte, T. 23/35, *s.* Lord. A.S. *drighten,* O. Icel. *drottin.*
Dronkelow, 84/67, *adj.* drunken, dissipated. " Drunkelew, *ebriosus.*"— Prompt. Parv.
Drouȝ, L. iii. 37/230, *v. pt. t.* dragd, tore. A.S. *dreogan.*
Dubbyng, 13/76, *s.* ornaments, decoration.
Dude, 88/214, *v. pt. t.* causd.
Duden, L. i. 19/19, *v. pt. t.* did.
Dure, L. i. 73/1084, *v.* endure, last.
Dwelle, V. 38/139, *v.* delay, stop.
Dyche, C. 53/258, *s.* dish.
Dyghte, L. iii. 21/12; Dyȝte, T. 21/12, *v. pt. t.* furnisht, prepared. A.S. *dihtan.*
Dyned, L. i. 46/561, *v. pt. t.* roard.
Dyngnytee, C. 63/320, *s.* rank, dignity.

Ede, V. 33/97, *v. pt. t.* went. A.S. *eode* = ivit.
Edissa, The city of, 32.
Eie, 85/131, *s.* awe, fear. Stode hem of hym non eie = stood in no fear of him.
Eire, L. i. 67/1031, *s.* heir.
Eke, T. 21/18, *adv.* a.so. A.S. *eac, ec.*
Elde, L. i. 25/136,·*s.* ag*, years. A.S. *eald, ald.*

Elijah raises Jonah, 86; burns up the messengers of King Ahaziah, 87; is taken up into heaven, 88.
Elisha purifies a well with salt, 88.
Elke, C. 28/79; Ilke, Ylke, *adj.* each, every.
Emforþ, 83/33, *v. imp.* (?) strengthen. O. Fr. *enforcer* renforcer, rendre plus fort.
Ene, L. i. 34/317, *adv.* once. A.S. *æne.*
Enk, L. i. 53/754, *s.* ink.
Enpaired, 84/66, *pp.* injurd.
Enpeirement, L. i. 32/255, *s.* injury, loss.
Entayele, C. 41/188, *s.* shape, form.
Entent, L. i. 39/412, *s.* purpose.
Enticement, L. i. 32/264, *s.* snares, allurements.
Eode, V. 48/261, *v. pt. t.* went.
Ere, 12/25, *s.* ear. A.S. *eare.*
Erley, C. 27/67; Erlich, L. i. 41/433, *adv.* early, soon. A.S. *earlice.*
Erþlich, 83/48, *adj.* worldly, earthly.
Euen 92/12, *adj.* level, flat.
Euenyng, V. 20/8; Euening, L. ii. 20/8, *s.* peer, equal. O. Icel. *iafningi.*
Euerichon, L. iii. 33/194, every one, all.
Eufemian (father of St. Alexius), p. 20, 21, 28, 37, 40, 48—51.
Euyne, C. 28/79, *s.* even, evening. A.S. *æfen.*
Eye, 87/173, *s.* awe, fear; A.S. *ege.* See Eie.
Eyled, L. iii. 27/108, *v. pt. t.* (?) no play, aild, troubled, him; he didn't care for it. T. has 'no play (in bed) easd them, the bridegroom and bride.'
Eyre, L. i. 23/112, *s.* heir.

Fairhede, L. i. 72/1080, *s.* beauty.
Fare, L. iii. 26/85; T. 26/85, *v.* go, travel. A.S. *faran.*
Fayne, C. 24/40, *adj.* glad, pleased. A.S. *fægen.*
Fe, T. 33/196; Feo, L. iii. 33/196, *s.* property. L. Lat. *feudum.*

Feble, L. i. 33/278, *adj.* poor, miserable.

Fede, T. 57/378; Feode, L. iii. 57/378, *v.* feed.

Feinte, 14/118, *v.* fall, be afraid.

Felawȝe, L. i. 35/329, *s.* fellow, companion. A.S. *felaga.*

Felawrede, L. i. 43/477, *s.* company, fellowhood.

Felde, C. 26/54, *sb.* field (? to manage loans and fields, business and agriculture).

Fele, C. 21/10, *adj.* many. A.S. *fela.*

Felede, V. 78/601, *v. pt. t.* experienced, met with.

Felle, C. 26/62, *adj.* many.

Felle, 96/166, *s.* skin. A.S. *fell*, Lat. *pellis.*

Fen, L. i. 45/527, *s.* mud. A.S. *fenn.*

Fend, T. 25/70; Feond, L. iii. 25/70, *s.* fiend, devil.

Fenge, T. 75/580; Fonge, L. iii. 75/580, *pp.* receivd, granted.

Feorliche, V. 73/546; Ferliche, L. ii. 73/546, *adj.* wonderful. A.S. *færlic*, sudden, from *fær* = sudden.

Ferd, V. 62/404, *v. pt. t.* fared, was.

Fere, L. iii. 25/59; T. 25/59, *s.* companions, schoolfellows.

Fere, 83/42, *s.* fear, respect.

Fette, L. i. 54/759, *v. pt. t.* fetcht.

Feye, L. iii. 73/555, *adj.* dead. A.S. *fæge.*

Fierþe, 85/100, *adj.* fourth. A.S. *feorðe.*

Fiȝth, L. i. 61/930, *s.* quarrelling, fighting.

Fle, T. 20/5; Fleo, L. iii. 20/5, *v.* flee from, resign. A.S. *fleon.*

Flene, L. i. 33/276, *v.* fly. A.S. *fleon.*

Fleschlich, 88/204, *adv.* in flesh.

Flynge, L. i. 68/1034, *v.* fling herself, rush.

Flyt, L. iii. 22/20, *s.* scolding, brawling. A.S *flit.*

Fo, L. iii. 72/539, *v.* take (clasp, embrace), A.S. *fon.*

Fode, L. iii. 23/29; T. 23/39, *s.* lit. food, hence, 'one brought up,' *alumnus*, finally = child, boy. A.S. *fóda.*

Follde, C. 56/267, *v. pt. t.* folded.

Fon, 83/37, *s. pl.* foes.

Fonde, 90/287, *v.* try, find out.

Fonding, L. iii. 28/119; Fondynge, T. 28/119, *s.* temptation, trial, perplexity.

Foot, 94/49, *s.* to foot and to honde = in every way.

Forbore, 94/69, *pp.* spared.

Force, C. 76/399, *s.* consideration, thought. Yaffe no force = took no notice.

Fordon, 86/160, *pp.* ruind.

Foresaweþ, 84/96, (?) *fore*, before; and *sawen*, to sow; or 'saws apart,' like *for-drifan*, drive asunder.

Forlore, L. iii. 30/158; T. 30/158, *pp.* lost, ruind.

Forsake, L. i. 64/964, *v.* refuse, deny.

Forsakyng, C. 39/155, *pp.* forsaken.

Forswelewed, 89/259, *pp.* swallowd utterly.

Forto, 95/125, *adv.* until.

Forto, T. 34/207, *adv.* until.

Forþer, 15/138, *adv.* fore, front.

Forþi, V. 35/112, *conj.* in order that.

Forȝete, L. iii. 67/479; Forȝute, T. 67/479, *v.* forget. A.S. *forgitan.*

Fourtide, 85/107, *adj.* fortieth. A.S. *feowertigoða.*

Fowlke, C. 57/272, *s.* folk, people. A.S. *folc.*

Frakel, L. iii. 44/279, *adj.* frail, fragile.

Frape, L. i. 60/390, *s.* crowd, numbers. O. Fr. *frape.*

Fre, T. 20/2, 20/4; Freo, L. iii. 20/2, 20/4, *adj.* free, noble.

Frel, T. 44/279, *adj.* frail, fickle. O. Fr. *frele, frail.*

Frenesie, L. i. 75/1112, *s.* madness.

Freond, L. iii. 72/545, *s.* a friend.

Frere, L. i. 61/928, *s.* friar, monk. Lat. *frater*.
Fryst, C. 72/375, *adj.* first.
Fyʒt, T. 22/20, *s.* fighting, quarrelling.
Fyn, L. iii. 26/90; Fyne, 94/56, *s.* ending, end of life. Fr. *fin*, Lat. *finis*.
Fyne, T. 26/90, *v.* end one's life, die.

Gaffe, C. 25/50, *v. pt. t.* gave. Gaffe he nought = took no heed, cared nought for.
Galys (Galicia), 32.
Game, L. i. 29/208, *s.* play.
Gamed, 95/120, *v. pt. t.* pleased.
Gange, L. ii. 25/44; Gonge, V. 25/44, *v.* walk. Scotch, *gang*.
Gascoyne, C. 28/78, *s.* Gascony.
Gate, L. ii. 33/98, *s.* road, way. Icel. *gata*.
Gate, C. 22/17, *s.* class, description. A.S. *geat*.
Gentel, T. 77/610; Gentyl, L. iii. 77/610, *adj.* noble.
Gest, C. 28/79, *s.* guest. A.S. *gæst, gest*.
Gete, V. 50/282, *v.* recover.
Gewyn, C. 41/182, *pp.* given.
Gile, 83/58, *v.* beguile, deceive.
Ginne, V. 62/412; Gyn, L. ii. 62/412, *s.* plan, means. Fr. *engin*, Lat. *ingenium*.
Gle, T. 27/106; Gleo, L. iii. 27/106, *s.* glee, merriment.
Glem, 12/27, *s.* gleam.
Godes, L. ii. 50/363; Godus, V. 58/362, *s.* of God.
Godspel, L. i. 19/34, *s.* Gospel.
Goed, L. iii. 21/17; Guod, T. 21/17, *adj.* good.
Gom, L. iii. 27/104; Gome, T. 27/104, *s.* man. A.S. *guma*.
Gonnen, L. i. 24/130, *v. pt. t.* began, settled. A.S. *ginnan*.
Gorre, L. i. 65/1005, *v. pt. t.* mud, dirt. A.S. *gor*.
Gostes, 93/44, *s. pl.* spirits. A.S. *gast*.

Gostlich, T. 25/72; Gostliche, L. iii. 25/72, *adv.* spiritually, in spirit.
Goþ, V. 38/142, *v. imper.* go.
Grad, L. i. 64/979, *v. pt. t.* read, spoke. Gradde, L. i. 36/364, cried. A.S. *grædan*.
Gram, L. iii. 60/406, *adj.* angry, annoyed. A.S. *gram*.
Gramed, L. i. 53/734, *v. pt. t.* grievd, annoyd. A.S. *gramian*.
Grede, L. iii. 53/340, *v.* cry. A.S. *grædan*.
Gredyng, 96/156, *v.* crying.
Greiþed, V. 78/596, *pp.* prepard.
Grene, L. i. 34/316, *adj.* green, fresh, sharp. Cp. verjuice, and Fr. *verd*, 'rawly tart or sharpe, as vnripe fruit, or wine,' &c.—Cotgrave.
Grente, L. iii. 36/217, *v. pt. t.* groaned.
Grete, L. i. 46/564, *v. pt. t.* wept. A.S. *grætan*.
Greth, L. ii. 24/40, *adj.* great.
Grette, L. ii. 48/296, *v. pt. t.* accosted, addrest.
Grijs, L. i. 38/398, *s.* the fur of the gray or martin.
Grikkissh, L. i. 47/591, *adj.* Grecian.
Grille, L. i. 46/564, *adv.* terribly. "Grym, gryl, *horridus*."—Prompt. Parv.
Griselich, 93/33, *adj.* fearful.
Grone, L. i. 39/414, *v.* groan, lament.
Grot, L. i. 47/608, *s.* lot, literally fragment. A.S. *grot*.
Grucchyng, L. i. 46/547, *s.* grumbling. O. Fr. *grouchier*.
Gylle, C. 25/55, *s.* guile, deceit.
Gynne, L. iii. 65/459, *s.* trick.
Gyrdell, C. 31/103, *s.* girdle.

Hab, 95/99, *v.* have.
Halewen, 12/44, *s. pl.* saints. A.S. *halig, haleg*, holy.
Halt, L. i. 61/931, *v. pt. t.* holds.
Haluendel, L. i. 35/334, *s.* half.
Halwe, L. iii. 75/582, *adv.* holy man, saint.

Ham-ward, V. 40/164, *adv.* homeward.
Happes, L. i. 69/1046, *s. pl.* fortune.
Hare, T. 22/23, *poss. pr.* their. A.S. *heor.*
Hast, L. i. 46/576, *s.* haste. On hast, in haste, very quickly.
Hatte, L. ii. 32/88 ; Hette, V. 32/88, *v. pt. t.* was named. A.S. *hatan.*
Haue, V. 76/581 ; Hawe, L. ii. 76/581, *s.* a haw, the berry of the hawthorn, equivalent here to our expression " not a fig."
Hawȝe, L. i. 35/328, *s.* yard or enclosure. A.S. *haga.* Chaucer uses it in the sense of a churchyard.
He, L. ii. 39/153, *pr.* they.
Hedde, L. ii. 57/358 ; Hudde, V. 57/358, *v. pt. t.* hid, coverd.
Heer, L. iii. 30/146 ; Her, T. 30/146, *s.* hair. A.S. *hær.*
Heiȝe, 15/139, *adj.* high, principal, noble.
Heiȝed, 95/98, *v. pt. t.* hied, hastend. A.S. *higian.*
Heiȝer, 92/4, *adj.* higher.
Heixt, 94/29, *adj.* highest. Ancren Riwle, pp. 42 and 138. Laȝamon, 1807, 2325 and 24,142.
Hele, L. iii. 29/127, *v.* conceal (his resolve).
Hele, 84/72, *v.* hide, cover. A.S. *helan.*
Helestou, L. iii. 67/476; Heleþou, T. 67/476, *v. pt. t.* didst thou hide. A.S. *helan.*
Hell, C. 77/412, *s.* cure, healing. A.S. *hæl.*
Hende, L. i. 21/81, *adj.* gentle, kind, polite. A.S. (ge)-*hende.*
Hende, L. i. 37/374, *adv.* near, at hand.
Hennes, L. i. 37/384, *adv.* hence. A.S. *heonan.*
Heo, V. 23/28, *pr.* she.
Heold, V. 62/409, *v. pt. t.* held.
Her, L. i. 53/731, *s.* hair-cloth.
Her, 90/292, of them. Her either after oþer = one of them after the other.
Herberewe, 93/40, *v.* harbour, shelter, lodge. " Herberwyn or receyvyn to hereboroghe, *hospitor.*"—Prompt. Parv.
Herd, V. 62/403, *pp.* heard.
Herde, V. 41/182, *s.* company, group.
Herede T. 39/250 ; Heried, L. iii. 39/250, *v. pt. t.* praisd, worshipt. A.S. *hérian.*
Herest, L. iii. 67/475, *v. pr. t.* hearest.
Herie, 93/4, *v.* praise, worship.
Herkynnythe, C. 20/2 ; Herkeneþ, T. 20/1, *v. imp.* hearken, listen.
Herne, L. i. 63/951, *s.* corner. O. Dutch, *herne.* " Hyrne, *angulus.*" —Prompt. Parv.
Herynge, T. 44/278, *s.* praise, honour.
Hest, L. i. 47/587, *s.* orders, command.
Hete, L. i. 60/904, *v. pt. t.* was named. A.S. *hatan.*
Hete, 86/153, *v. pt. t.* orderd, commanded. A.S. *hatan.*
Hetilich, 11/15, *adv.* hatefully, spitefully. A.S. *hetelice.*
Heþingge, L. ii. 52/308, *s.* contempt, mockery.
Heu, L. iii. 27/99 ; Hewe, T. 27/99, *s.* complexion. A.S. *heow.*
Heuede, 13/59, *s.* head. A.S. *heafod.*
Heuenriche, 14/108, *s.* of heaven. A.S. *heofonrice.*
Hide, L. i. 52/713, *s.* features. A.S. *hyd.*
Hiȝte, V. 22/25 ; Hihte, V. 21/9 ; Hyȝtte, L. ii. 22/25, *v. pt. t.* was named. A.S. *hatan.*
Hij, 11/16, *pr.* they. A.S. *hi.*
Hol, 83/38, *adv.* safe, whole. A.S. *hal.*
Hom, V. 42/193, *s.* man, servant.
Honden, 14/95, *s. pl.* hands. A.S. *hond.*
Hore, L. iii. 36/218, *adj.* white, hoary.
Hosebonde, 88/224, *s.* husband.
Hote, L. i. 43/488, *v. pr. t.* bid, order. A.S. *hatan.*
Hou, L. i. 19/48, *adv.* how.

Houseled, L. i. 35/337, *pp.* receivd the Sacrament. A.S. *huslian*.

Housles, 93/40, *adj.* houseless, homeless.

Hungred, L. i. 35/335, *pp.* of hungred = exceedingly hungry, from A.S. *ofhingrian*.

Hure, 13/59, *s.* cap. "*Howe* or *hure*, heed hyllynge, Tena, capedulum."—Prompt. Parv.

Hy, T. 22/22, *pr.* they.

Hye, C. 69/362, *adv.* on hye = aloud, in a loud voice.

Hylde, C. 52/257, *v. pt. t.* coverd. A.S. *hilan*.

Hyllde, C. 63/315, *v. pt. t.* held, kept.

Hynde, C. 64/340, *adv.* kindly, gently.

Hyne, L. iii. 31/176, *s.* attendant. A.S. *hina*.

Hywe, T. 28/117, *s.* complexion, colour. A.S. *heow*.

Ibe, 89/253, *pp.* been.

Icham, 97/28, I am.

Ichaue, V. 71/508, *v. pr. t.* I have.

Icholde, V. 71/521, *v. pr. t.* for I wolde = I wish, I would.

I-herid, L. ii. 40/157, *pp.* praisd. A.S. *hêrian*.

Ihote (11/5), *pp.* calld, named. A.S. *hatan*.

Ilche, V. 43/210; Ilk, L. ii. 43/210, *adj.* same, very one.

In, 97/33; Inne, V. 67/459, *s.* house, residence.

Innocent, Pope, enquires about St. Alexius, 60; receives the book from Alexius, 64.

Ireful, 82/20, *adj.* wrathful.

Iryde, 89/250, *pp.* ridden, been carried.

Ised, 92/22, *pp.* said, told.

Isen, 95/140, *v. pt. t.* have seen.

I-seȝen, V. 70/493, *pp.* seen.

Iwisse, 92/24, *adv.* certainly, assuredly. O. Fris. *wis*, Icel. *viss*, Dutch, *gewis* = certain.

Jerome's, St., Fifteen Tokens before Doomsday, p. 92.

Jonah swallowed by a whale, 47, 48.

Judgment of Solomon, 98.

Kee, C. 68/358, *s.* for "knee."

Ken, V. 33/96; Kenne, L. ii. 33/96, *v.* know, recognise. A.S. *cunnan*.

Kende, 86/154, *v. pt. t.* became acquainted with. A.S. *cunnan*.

Kene, 96/6, *adj.* angry.

Kenne, T. 27/99; Kinne, L. iii. 27/99, *s.* family, race.

Kepte, L. iii. 44/278, *v. pt. t.* regarded, valued. A.S. *cêpan*.

Kesse, T. 67/480, *v.* kiss.

Kete, L. iii. 33/201, *adj.* strong.

Kiþe, L. i. 30/224, *v.* show, make known. A.S. *cýðan, cuðian*.

Knaue, C. 27/69, *s.* servant, dependant.

Kneuȝ, V. 67/456, *v. pt. t.* knew, recognised.

Knouyng, L. i. 33/275, *s.* knowledge, recognition.

Knwe, C. 41/177, *v. pt. t.* knew, recognised.

Kyd, L. iii. 61/410, *adj.* known, recognised. A.S. *cuð*.

Kynde, L. i. 20/49, *s.* kin, family, nature. A.S. *cun*.

Kyndes, 85/130, *s. pl.* tribes.

Kyngesday, 86/147, *s.* days, time or reign of King Ahab.

Kyngus, V. 20/8, *s.* of a king.

Kynrede, L. i. 22/93, *s.* family.

Lafdy, 14/91, *s.* lady.

Laodicea, St Alexius arrives at, 45.

Lask, L. i. 50/681, *v.* alleviate.

Lauedye, L. iii. 23/33; Leuedye, T. 23/33, *s.* lady.

Lauȝtte, L. i. 30/219, *v. pt. t.* came upon, seizd. A.S. *læccan*.

Lawe, 85/126, *v.* put down, subdue.

Lawȝes, L. i. 54/748, *s. pl.* laws.

Leccherie, 84/68, *s.* dissipation, indulgence. "Lechery, *luxuria, fornicatio*."—Prompt. Parv.

Leche, V. 28/59, *s.* physician, curer. A.S. *læce*.

INDEX OF WORDS AND SUBJECTS.   111

Led, C. 26/56, *v.* spend, pass.
Led, V. 66/444, *s.* lead.
Ledes, L. i. 23/111, *s. pl.* people, dependants. A.S. *leod.*
Lees, C. 68/354, net, snare. O. Fr. *las, lays,* a snare, ginne, or grinne. —Cotgrave.
Lees, C. 22/20 ; Les, V. 22/26, *s.* lying, a lie. A.S. *leas,* false.
Leet, L. i. 32/268, *v. pt. t.* gave up, resignd. A.S. *lettan.*
Leffe, C. 66/439, *adj.* dear. A.S. *leof.*
Lefnesse, L. i. 48/627, *s.* faith. "Levenesse or belevenesse, *fides.*"— Prompt. Parv.
Legge, 98/46, *v.* appease, settle.
Leȝe, V. 57/358, *v. pt. t.* lay.
Leiden, 11/15, *v. pt. t.* laid on, pressed on.
Leie, 87/188, flame. A.S. *leg, lig.*
Leinte, 14/117, *s.* the season of Lent.
Lele, L. ii. 75/567, *adj.* whole, sound.
Lem, T. 64/439 ; Leom, L. iii. 64/439, *s.* ray of light, beam.
Leman, T. 29/130 ; Lemman, L. iii. 29/130, *s.* sweetheart, love. A.S. *leofman.*
Leneden, 89/244, *v. pt. t.* lay, leant.
Lengþe, L. i. 25/136, *s.* stature, height.
Lepy, T. 36/215, *adj.* single. O lepy = anlepy = a single. A.S. *anlepig.*
Ler, L. iii. 37/232 ; Lere, T. 37/232, *v.* teach, tell. A.S. *leornian.*
Lere, L. iii. 28/122 ; T. 28/112, *s.* countenance. A.S. *hleor,* O. Icel. *hlýr.*
Lere, V. 25/45 ; L. ii. 25/45 ; Lore, L. iii. 24/54 ; T. 24/54, *s.* learning, school.
Leryd, C. 58/281, *adj.* learned.
Les, 15/147, *s.* lying, lies.
Lest, L. i. 47/595, *v. pt. t.* lasted.
Lest, 92/24, *adj.* least, smallest. A.S. *læst.*
Letanye, L. i. 57/830, *s.* a litany.
Lete, L. i. 28/181, *v. pt. t.* set aside, gave up, restraind. A.S. *lettan.*

Leten, L. ii. 74/548, *v. pt. t.* causd.
Lette, 15/123, *v.* be prevented, stop. A.S. *lettan.*
Leue, 14/92, *adj.* dear, beloved.
Leue, 14/99, *s.* leave, permission.
Leued, 85/132, *v. pt. t.* remaind, were left.
Leuen, L. iii. 29/132, *v.* live, remain.
Leuer, L. i. 27/172, *adv.* rather, sooner.
Leuyde, C. 67/346, *pp.* left.
Lewde, C. 58/281, *adj.* unlearned.
Lewe, C. 71/369, *adj.* dear.
Lewe, C. 31/101, *v.* live, remain.
Libbe, L. i. 55/792, *v.* live.
Liche, L. iii. 70/512 ; Lich, T. 70/512, *s.* body. A.S. *lic.* "Lyche, dead body, *funus.*"—Prompt. Parv.
Lift, L. iii. 56/371 ; Luft, T. 56/371, *s.* air ; bi the lift = aloft, on high.
Liȝe, 84/87, *v.* lie. A.S. *leogan.*
Liȝth, L. i. 19/6, *adj.* active.
Liȝth, 87/188, *adj.* light, burning.
Liȝttyng, 93/25, *s.* lightning. A.S. *lýhtinge.*
Liggande, V. 63/420 ; Liggynde, L. ii. 63/420, *pr. p.* lying.
Liht, V. 23/36 ; Lyȝthe, L. ii. 23/36, *v.* lighten, comfort. A.S. *lihtan.*
Lijf, L. i. 26/147 ; Lyffe, C. 26/56, *s.* life.
Limes, V. 75/567 ; Lymes, L. ii. 75/567, *s. pl.* limbs.
Liþer, 83/60, *adj.* rascally, wicked. A.S. *lyðer.*
Liþerhede, 88/218, *s.* badness, impurity.
Liuesman, L. iii. 63/430, *s.* a living man.
Llawe, C. 51/253, *adj.* low.
Lombe, 15/138, *s.* lamb.
Look, L. i. 50/674, *v.* attend to.
Loos, L. i. 44/499, *s.* praise, glory. O. Fr. *los,* Lat. *laus.*
Lordingges, L. ii. 59/383 ; Lordingus, V. 59/383, *s. pl.* Sirs.
Lothe, C. 36/132, *adj.* loath, troublesome, sorrow-causing.

Lovde, 84/87, *adv.* loudly.
Loueden, L. i. 19/3, *v. pt. t.* loved.
Louelich, 14/93. *adj.* lovely.
Louke, L. iii. 77/611, *v.* enclose. A.S. *lucan* = to lock.
Lousse, C. 63/321, *s.* loose.
Lowe, C. 41/174, *s.* love.
Lowthe, C. 42/195, *v.* bow, kneel. A.S. *hlútan.*
Lowyght, C. 77/414, *v. pr. t.* loveth.
Luþer, T. 61/409, *adj.* wretched, vile. A.S. *lyðer.*
Lyte, a, V. 75/561, *adv.* a little, a bit.
Lywyd, C. 40/168, *v. pr. t.* lived.

Maistrie, 13/85, *s.* the mastery, victory.
Make, V. 37/130, *s.* mate, partner. O. Icel. *maki.*
Mangery, C. 26/63, *s.* feast, banquet. Fr. *mangeoir.*
Manyon. L. iii. 30/155; T. 30/155, many a one.
Marriage of St. Alexius, 27.
Maryole, L. i. 43/481, *s.* little Mary, little image. Lat. *mariola.*
May, L. iii. 28/116; T. 28/116, *s.* maiden. A.S. *mæg.*
Me, V. 44/228, men, people.
Mechul, V. 44/220; Muchel, L. ii. 44/220, *adj.* much, great.
Mede, T. 57/375; Meode, L. iii. 57/375, *s.* reward. A.S. *med.*
Meignee, L. i. 61/914, *s.* servants, household. See Meyny.
Melys, C. 35/126, *s.* meal.
Mende, L. i. 33/271, *s.* mind, thoughts.
Mendement, 96/152, *s.* improvement, help.
Mene, L. i. 40/421, *v.* lament.
Menee, L. i. 60/903, *s.* retinue, attendants. See Meyny.
Menge, L. iii. 48/299, *r.* think, remember. A.S. *myngian.*
Menged, L. iii. 28/118, *v. pt. t.* became confusd or disturbd. A.S. *mencgan*, mix ; O.L. Ger. *mengian.*
Menske, L. i. 74/1098, *s.* honour, reverence. O. Icel. *menska.*

Meschief, L. i. 36/353, *s.* trouble, misery.
Messe, L. i. 56/877, *s.* Mass.
Mest, 93/37, *adj.* especially.
Mester, V. 51/300.
Mesure, 13/60 *s.* measure. A measure = fitting, suitable. Fr. *à mesure.*
Met, C. 35/123, *s.* meat, food. A.S. *mete.*
Mette, 11/3, *v. pt. t.* dreamt. A.S. *mætan.*
Metyng, 12/42, *s.* dream.
Meyny, C. 47/232, *s.* servants, household. O. Fr. *maisne* = household, from L. Lat. *maisnada* (from Lat. *minus natu*), a company; cf. *menials.*
Mid, 83/53, *prep.* with. A.S. *mid.*
Middelerd, 92/18, *s.* earth.
Miracles wrought by the corpse of Alexius, 75.
Misse, 92/23, *s.* lose, be without.
Misseist, 84/71, *v. pr. t.* say against, annoy.
Mist, V. 71/511, *v. pt. t.* mightest.
Miȝtten, 11/16, *aux. v.* might, could.
Mode, L. 19/26 ; T. 60/404; Moed, L. iii. 60/404, *s.* spirit, heart, mind. A.S. *mód.*
Molde, L. i. 21/83, *s.* earth. A.S. *molde.*
Mon, C. 23/28 ; L. ii. 23/32 ; Mone, V. 23/32, *s.* lamentation.
Mone, 83/53, *s.* 'non In mone,' (?) no mention, or 'no share,' community.
Moneþ, 12/38, *s. pl.* months. A.S. *monað.*
Monnes, V. 26/50, *s.* man's ; Monnus, V. 45/230, *pl.* men's.
Morenyng, C. 40/157, *s.* mourning, lamentation.
Mot, L. iii. 29/131 ; L. 29/131, *aux. v.* must.
Mote, 14/101, *aux. v.* may.
Mowen, L. i. 39/409, *aux. v.* may.
Murre, 15/140, murry, mulberry-coloured, red-purple.
Mychel, 11/4, *adj.* much, great.
Myd, 11/12, *prep.* with. A.S. *mid.*

INDEX OF WORDS AND SUBJECTS. 113

Myddellerede, 16/167; Mydlerde, 92/19, earth. A.S. *middeleard*.
Mydeward, L. ii. 74/551, midst.
Myldelich, 82/21, *adv*. mildly.
Mysse, 97/30, *v*. miss, fail.
Mystook, L. i. 22/94, *v. pt. t.* transgrest, offended.
Mytred, 13/79, *pp*. with a mitre on.
Mytte, 83/43, *prep*. with. A.S. *mid*. Goth. *miþ*.

Nadde, L. iii. 24/49; T. 24/49 for 'ne hadde' = had not.
Nam, T. 31/169, *v. pt. t.* took. A.S. *niman*.
Namelich, 84/93, *adv*. especially.
Narewe, L. i. 61/932; Narewȝ, 95/99, *adv*. closely, nearly, narrowly, in small compass.
Nas, 85/118, for 'ne was' = was not.
Naþeles, L. i. 28/181, *adv*. nevertheless.
Naþemo, 94/41, *adv*. nothing more.
Neb, L. iii. 63/434; Nebbe, L. iii. 52/330, *s*. head, face.
Nedliche, V. 35/116, *adv*. necessarily.
Neiȝ, T. 63/436; Neyȝ, L. iii. 63/436, *adv*. near, nigh.
Neiȝe, V. 70/487; Neyh, L. ii. 70/487, *v*. approach. A.S. *nehwan*.
Nempned, 12/45, *pp*. named, mentioned. A.S. *nemnan*. Lat. *nominare*.
Nere, L. iii. 30/150; T. 30/150, for 'ne were' = was not, were not.
Nest, V. 56/339, *adj*. next.
Newed, V. 73/539, *pp*. renewed.
Newfangel, 83/35, *adj*. new-fangled, new, inconstant.
Ney, L. iii. 25/56; Neȝ, T. 25/56, *adj*. near, nigh. A.S. *neh*, *neah*.
Niht, V. 23/33; Nyȝthe, L. ii. 23/33, *s*. night.
Nineveh, 47.
Niste, L. iii. 53/332; Nuste, T. 53/332, *v. pt. t.* for 'ne wiste,' *i. e.* did not know of.
ADAM DAVY

Nolde, L. i. 29/202, for 'ne wolde' = would not.
Nom, 13/58, *v. pt. t.* took, directed. A.S. *niman*.
Nome, L. iii. 76/605, *s*. name.
None kynnes, L. i. 33/274, no manner. See 'Scunes.'
Noot, L. i. 39/419, for 'ne wot' = do not know.
Noue, C. 37/144, *adv*. now.
Nouȝth, 14/118, *adv*. not.
Nowar, L. ii. 58/372; Nower, 95/131, *adv*. nowhere. A.S. *nâhwer*, for *ne âhwer*.
Nowder, C. 27/69, neither.
Nowgth, 96/5; Nowth, L. ii. 53/92, *adv*. nought, not.
Nyll, 84/72, for 'ne wyll' = will not.
Nyllen, 97/44, for 'ne wyllen' = are not willing.
Nyltou, L. i. 66/1017, for 'ne wylt thou' = wilt thou not.
Nyme, 89/257, *v*. take, be taken.
Nysten, 95/78, for 'ne wysten' = did not know.

Obedde, L. iii. 22/23, *adv*. to bed.
Oftesiþes, V. 70/479, *adv*. oftentimes.
Oiþer, L. i. 75/1112, *conj*. or.
On, L. i. 28/191, *num*. one; on & on = one by one.
Ou bynde, C. 64/341, *v. pt. t.* opened.
Onon, 12/23, *adv*. presently, anon.
Oo, L. i. 41/442, *num. adj*. one.
Oord, L. i. 54/763; Orde, L. i. 78/1141, *s*. beginning.
Oord, L. i. 29/200, the edge or point. A.S. *ord*.
Opbreyde, T. 30/155; Vpbreed, L. iii. 30/155, *v*. upbraid, abuse, blame.
Ordre, L. i. 22/86, *s*. a religious order.
Ore, L. iii. 36/220, *s*. mercy, pity.
Orn, L. iii. 69/510, *v*. run, flow;
Ornen, V. 75/560, *pt. t.* ran.
Ost, L. i. 64/981, *s*. company. O. Fr. *host*.
Oþer while, L. iii. 31/173, sometimes.
Oþer, 92/5, that oþer dai = the next

8

INDEX OF WORDS AND SUBJECTS.

or the second day; cf. Havelok, l. 1755 (ed. Skeat), þe oþer day.

Ou, V. 31/73, *pr.* you.

Ouerlay, 97/35, *v. pt. t.* lay on, smothered.

Oune, L. ii. 48/300; Owene, T. 48/300, *adj.* own.

Ouse, L. i. 50/672, *v.* use.

Outgan, L. iii. 63/431, *pp.* departed.

Outwinne, L. iii. 64/450, *v.* get (it) out.

Ouȝtten, 94/40, *v. pr. t.* ought, owe.

Owe, L. i. 49/643, *adj.* own, his owe = his own parents, friends.

Oxse, T. 21/11, *s. pl.* oxen. A.S. *oxa.* Gothic, *auhsa.*

Paie. L. i. 35/324, *v.* please. See Paye.

Pais, 98/54, *s.* peace. Fr. *paix.* Lat. *pacem.*

Pal, L. iii. 74/566; Palle, T. 74/366, *s.* fine cloth. Lat. *pallium.*

Palesye, L. i. 75/1111, *s.* palsy.

Palfreies, L. i. 23/114, *s. pl.* riding-horses. Fr. *palefroi.*

Paraile, L. i. 27/165, *s.* dress.

Paraile, L. i. 56/810, *s.* make, trim.

Parchemyne, L. i. 53/754, *s.* parchment, paper. Fr. *parchemin.*

Parde, 95/102 = par dieu = by god.

Partener, L. ii. 58/365; Partinere, V. 58/365, *s.* partner, sharer. L. Lat. *partionarius.*

Party, L. i. 37/384, *v.* depart. Fr. *partir.*

Pas, L. iii. 24/41, *s.* steps. Lat. *passus.*

Passeþ, 83/37, *v. pr. t.* appeases, overcomes.

Paye, C. 27/66, *v.* please; welle to paye = so as to please greatly. Lat. *pacare.*

Pece, C. 27/75, *s.* a drinking cup. — Palsgrave. *Cateria,* Anglice, a *pese.*—Nominale MS.

Peines, L. iii. 29/134; Peynes, T. 29/134, *s. pl.* pains, troubles.

Pelured, L. i. 38/398, *adj.* trimmed with fur.

Pendaunt, C. 21/12, *s.* Fr. '*Pendant :* m. a pendant; a hanger; any thing that hangeth, or whereat another thing hangs.'—Cotgrave.

Pens, L. i. 31/247, *s.* pence, money.

Perchement, C. 63/314, *s.* writing.

Pere, L. i. 42/468, *adj.* equal.

Pilerinage, 14/103, *s.* pilgrimage. Fr. *pélerinage,* from Lat. *peregrinus,* a pilgrim.

Pine, L. iii. 30/159; Pyne, T. 30/159, *s.* pain, trouble.

Pite, 88/226, *v.* put.

Plawe, L. iii. 31/168, *s.* pleasure, amusement.

Plede, 83/51, *v. imper.* go to law.

Pleyn, 87/172, *s.* plain.

Pliȝt, V. 29/62; Plyȝth, L. ii. 29/62, *s.* danger. A.S. *pliht.*

Plouh, L. iii. 21/11; Plouȝ, T. 21/11, *s.* ploughs. O. Icel. *plôgr.* O. Dutch, *ploeg.*

Pormen, C. 22/16, *s. pl.* poor men.

Pouere, L. i. 20/59, *adj.* poor.

Pouste, L. 20/56, *s.* power, authority. Lat. *potestas.*

Prece, C. 75/394, *s.* press, crowd.

Preced, V. 77/583; Preceden, L. i. 77/583; Preseden, L. ii. 77/586, *v. pt. t.* prest, crowded.

Preijs, L. i. 38/397, *s.* value. Lat. *pretium.*

Prestes, C. 26/62, *s. pl.* priests. A.S. *preost.* O. Fr. *prestre.*

Presyowse, C. 62/306, *adj.* precious.

Preȝere, V. 52/304, *s.* prayer.

Priueli, V. 32/80, *adv.* privately, secretly.

Puruyaunce, L. i. 26/148, *s.* provision.

Puruyde, C. 26/55, *v. pt. t.* provided, found.

Pylte, L. i. 48/623, *v. pt. t.* pushed up.

Pymente, C. 27/72, piment, a drink made of spiced wine or ale.—See Halliwell, *s. v.* Piment.

INDEX OF WORDS AND SUBJECTS. 115

Queintise, 82/5, *s.* cleverness, knowledge.
Queme, L. iii. 52/321, *s.* to queme= at his pleasure.
Quene, 98/45, *s.* woman. A.S. *cwen.* Greek, γυνή.
Quik, V. 61/396, *adj.* alive, living. A.S. *cwic.*
Rad, L. i. 64/980, *v. pt. t.* read. A.S. *rédan.*
Radden, 85/116, *v. pt. t.* advised, counselled. A.S. *rædan.*
Raply, C. 68/353, *adj.* quick, speedy. Cf. Lat. *rapere* = to snatch.
Rauʒtte, L. i. 30/225, *v. pt. t.* handed, gave. A.S. *ræcan.*
Rebauudrye, C. 52/255 (alter *n* to *u* in the text), *s.* ribaldry.
Recke, L. iii. 73/552; Reiche, T. 73/552, *v. pr. t.* care, reck.
Red, L. i. 27/173, *s.* plan, course. A.S. *ræd.*
Red, L. i. 67/1025, *s.* A.S. *ræd,* 1. counsel, 2. advantage, benefit, reward.
Redly, C. 65/329, *adv.* plainly. A.S. *rædlice,* reasonably.
Reed, 85/118, *s.* advice, counsel.
Rehoboam made king, 85.
Reindropes, 82/11, *s. pl.* drops of rain.
Relyke, C. 74/392, *s.* relic.
Remeþ, T. 69/505, *v. imper.* make room for, clear away from. A.S. *ryman.*
Rent, L. i. 35/327, *pp.* torn, to-rent = torn to pieces.
Repmen, 89/246, *s. pl.* reapers.
Rese, C. 68/353, *s.* haste.
Reue, 93/4, *v.* take away.
Reuly, L. ii. 66/447, *adj.* pitiable, grievous.
Reuthe, L. iii. 59/398; Ruthe, T. 59/398, *s.* pity.
Rewe, L. i. 29/201, *v.* grieve, trouble. A.S. *hreowan.*
Rewe, 12/31, *s.* row, order, by rewe = in a line, in order. A.S. *raw.*
Rewely, L. i. 31/236, *adv.* woefully.

Righte, L. iii. 75/578 : Riʒt, T. 75/578, *v.* be healed, cured.
Rijf, L. iii. 26/156, *adj.* plenty, numerous.
Rochell, C. 28/78, *s.* Rochelle. "Rynische wyne and Rochelle."—Morte Arthure, E. E. Text Soc., Ed. Brock, p. 7, l. 203.
Rod, V. 69/476, Rode, 14/93, *s.* the rood, cross.
Rody, L. i. 60/941, *adj.* ruddy.
Rolle, C. 65/327, *s.* roll, writing.
Rome, 20, 35, 36, 45, 58.
Ron, V. 62/404, *v. pt. t.* ran, hurried.
Rood, 13/55, *v. pt. t.* rode. A.S. *ridan.*
Ros, L. iii. 29/42, *v. pt. t.* arose, recovered.
Rote, 82/13, *s.* root, foundation, beginning.
Roted, L. i. 38/408, 50/684, *pp.* rotted.
Roum, V. 69/481, *s.* room, place.
Route, T. 25/71, *s.* course, condition.
Royn (The River), 45.
Rymes in Solomon's *Book of Wonders,* p. 81.
Ryue, L. i. 52/720, *adj.* full, abounding.
Ryuere, L. i. 65/988, *s.* river-sports; hawking at the river-side; flying hawks at water-fowl.

Saiʒ, V. 71/522; Saye, L. ii. 71/522, *v. pt. t.* saw.
Sake, 14/90, *s.* guilt, sin.
Sarasynes, 14/86, *s. pl.* Saracens, pagans.
Sauh, V. 33/94, *v pt. t.* saw.
Sawʒe, L. i. 37/393, *s.* proverb, saw. A.S. *sagu.*
Say, L. ii. 31/73, *v. pt. t.* said, told.
Scee, C. 66/334, *v. pt. t.* see.
Schent, 84/95, *v. pr. t.* ruins, disgraces.
Schipes, V. 32/79, *s. pl.* ships. A.S. *scyp.*
Schome, V. 20/5, *s.* shame, disgrace.
Schride, 93/39, *v.* clothe. A.S. *scrydan.*
Schulder, 85/124, *s.* shoulder. A.S. *sculdor.*

Scunes, V. 62/412, Non scunes = nonnes kunes = no manner, no kind. See note to l. 219 of Joseph of Arimathie.
Seche, 92/14, v. seek, find.
Seeten, 33/98, v. pt. t. sat.
Segge, 88/203, v. pt. t. said.
Sei, V. 31/73; Seien, 84/86, v. pt. t. said, told. A.S. *secgan*.
Sekande, V. 39/145, *pr. p.* Sekynde, seeking.
Seke, L. iii. 21/13; Sike, T. 21/13, *adj.* sick folk.
Seld, L. iii. 33/194, v. pt. t. sold.
Selde, 94/24, *adv.* seldom. A.S. *seld*.
Selly, L. ii. 34/104, *s.* blessed object, relic. See Celli.
Semblaunt, 83/43, *s.* appearance, looks.
Sen, L. i. 25/142, v. see. A.S. *scon*.
Separation of the kingdoms of Israel and Judah, 85.
Serieauntz, L. i. 42/452, *s. pl.* attendants. Lat. *servientes*.
Serued, 14/108, *pp.* deserved.
Seruy, L. iii. 79/634, v. serve, worship.
Serwe, V. 60/441, *s.* grief.
Seueniȝth, 89/253, *s.* a week, seven nights.
Seuenteþe, L. ii. 54/325, *adj.* seventeenth.
Sexteyene, C. 42/192; Sextayne, C. 43/203, *s.* sacristan (sexton).
Sey, L. ii. 33/94, v. pt. t. saw. A.S. *seon*.
Seyetȝ, L. ii. 36/122, v. pr. t. sighs.
Shene, L. i. 26/154, *adj.* shining, beautiful.
Shent, L. i. 27/177, *pp.* ruined, disgraced. A.S. *sceandan*.
Shilde, 14/90, v. *imp.* shield, protect. A.S. *scildan*.
Shille, L. i. 46/550, 561, *adv.* shrilly.
Sho, 13/61, *s. pl.* shoes.
Shonde, L. iii. 26/80; T. 20/80, *s.* disgrace. A.S. *sccand, sceond*.
Shone, L. iii. 30/161; Shonye, T. 30/161, v. shun, avoid.

Shoures, L. 19/36, *s. pl.* conflicts, struggles. A.S. *scûr*.
Shred, L. iii. 28/126; Y-shrud, T. 28/126, *pp.* clad.
Shrewen, L. i. 46/572, *adj.* wicked.
Shride, L. iii. 74/565; Shrude, T. 74/565, shrouded. A.S. *scrydan*
Shroud, T. 36/218, *s.* clothes.
Shryuen, L. i. 35/338, *pp.* shriven, absolved. A.S. *scrifan*.
Sigge, V. 22/26, v. say. A.S. *secgan*.
Sike, L. iii. 51/315, v. sigh.
Sikeþ, V. 36/122, v. *pr. t.* sighs.
Sikerliche, V. 59/383; Sikerly, L. ii. 59/313, *adv.* assuredly, certainly. Lat. *secure*.
Siking, V. 66/449; Syking, L. ii. 66/449, *s.* sighing.
Sithen, L. iii. 26/88; Suþþe, T. 26/88, *adv.* afterwards.
Siȝte, T. 28/121; Syȝte, L. iii. 28/121, v. pt. t. sighed.
Skars, L. i. 46/560, *adj.* scarce, little. O. Fr. *escars*.
Skeet, L. i. 44/493, *adv.* quickly, speedily. O. Icel. *skiotr*.
Skil, V. 76/579; Skyl, L. ii. 76/579, *s.* reason, purpose.
Skorninge, V. 52/308, *s.* mockery.
Skript, L. ii. 62/409; Skrit, V. 62/409, *s.* writing.
Slake, L. ii. 57/354, v. cease, end, lessen.
Sle, 86/150, v. slay. A.S. *slean*.
Slowȝen, 86/136, v. pt. t. slew. A.S. *slean*, pt. t. *ic sloh*.
Smelde, L. ii. 78/601, v. pt. t. smelt.
Smerte, L. i. 33/281, *s.* suffering, pain.
Snell, L. iii. 38/240; Snelle, T. 38/240, *adv.* quickly, at once. A.S. *snell*.
So, 12/27, *conj.* as.
Soft, 95/92; Softe, L. i. 19/32, *adv.* easily, gently.
Soioure, L. i. 74/1101, *s.* delay, stopping.
Soke, L. i. 69/1045, v. pt. t. didst suck.

INDEX OF WORDS AND SUBJECTS. 117

Solomon, his love of lechery, 85; succeeded by Rehoboam, 85; his coronation, 97; his judgment, 98.
Somony, 97/1, v. summon; lete somony = caused to be summoned.
Sond, V. 32/82, s. land, shore.
Sonde, L. i. 31/239, s. message.
Sonenday, L. i. 56/817, s. Sunday.
Sonne-bem, 12/28, s. sunbeam, ray of the sun.
Soriere, L. iii. 70/518; Sorwere, T. 70/518, adj. more grieved.
Sorouȝeyng, L. i. 66/1011, s. Sorrow, grief.
Sorouȝfuleich, L. i. 68/1036, adv. piteously.
Soþlich, 15/132, adv. in truth, truly. A.S. soþlice.
Soulde, C. 26/56, aux. v. should, might.
South, L. ii. 74/554; Souȝth, L. i. 33/273, pp. sought for.
Souȝtten, L. i. 55/777, v. pt. t. sought.
Sowe, L. i. 33/282, v. pt. t. saw.
Sowen, V. 76/577, pp. scatterd, thrown about.
Speire, L. i. 67/1030, s. hope, wish. Lat. sperare.
Spelye, T. 35/208, v. spare. Occurs in Ormulum, 1. 10133.
Speten, 93/45, v. spit out.
Spicerie, V. 78/603; Spiserye, L. ii. 78/603, s. spices.
Spille, 16/156, v. to kill. A.S. spillan.
Sposaile, L. i. 26/159, s. betrothal.
Spousehode, 85/105, s. marriage, matrimony.
Spousyde, C. 26/60, pp. betrothd.
Spreusse, C. 45/220, s. Prussia.
Springe, V. 44/223, v. spread.
Sse, C. 31/106, s. the sea.
Stant, 84/84, v. pr. t. stands.
Stap, T. 69/503, v. pt. t. stept, walkt.
Stedes, L. i. 23/114, s. pl. steeds, horses. A.S. stêda.
Stel, 11/8, s. steel. A.S. style.

Stephene, L. ii. 43/202, s. voice. A.S. stefne.
Steren, 92/16, s. pl. stars. "Sterre, stella."—Prompt. Parv.
Steuene, L. i. 19/11, s. voice. A.S. stefne.
Stillelich, 84/85, adv. quietly.
Stiȝe, 93/26, v. pt. t. ascended. A.S. stégan, to mount. Prov. Eng. stee = a ladder. Cf. Eng. stirrup, i.e. sti-rop, a rope to mount by, stair, and stile.
Stod, T. 64/439; Stoed, L. iii. 64/439, v. pt. t. stood, issued.
Stout, L. ii. 61/401, s. (generally "sturt ne strif") daring, challenging, quarrelling. E.E. Stout, audax.
Strangli, 89/243, v. strangle, seize by the throat, kill, slay.
Stretford-atte-bowe, 14/113; Stretforþe-bowe, 16/164, Chaucer's Stratford-atte-Bow, in the East of London.
Strijf, L. i. 39/419, s. trouble.
Striueden, 97/38, v. pt. t. strove, contended.
Stronde, L. iii. 32/183, s. shore.
Stude, V. 45/231, s. place.
Sturte, V. 62/410, v. pt. t. started, hurried.
Stynge, L. i. 66/1017, v. sting, strike.
Suete, L. iii. 29/138, adj. sweet, dear.
Sumdel, 95/89, s. some.
Sumdel, L. i. 62/941, adv. somewhat, rather.
Sunne, V. 28/59, s. sin. A.S. synn.
Surrie (Syria), 33.
Sustene up, 97/14, inf. uphold.
Swalewe, L. i. 47/611, v. pt. t. swallowed.
Swaþel, T. 28/116, swa pel, so.
Swein, V. 48/263, s. attendant.
Swete, L. ii. 78/601; Swote, V. 78/601, adj. sweet.
Sweuene, 11/2, s. a dream. A.S swefen.
Swingge, L. ii. 66/443, slap, flat (down to the ground).

8 *

Swiþe, 11/17, *adv.* very, exceedingly, quickly.
Swounynge, L. iii. 29/142; Swoȝenynge, T. 29/142, *s.* swoon, faint.
Swoȝeny, T. 36/222; Swoune, L. iii. 36/222, *v.* faint, swoon.
Swynke, C. 57/275, *v.* labour, work. A.S. *swincan*.
Sylffe, C. 35/128, self.
Sylvyr, C. 76/397, *s.* silver, money.
Sythyn, C. 24/37, *adv.* afterwards, thenceforward.
Syttynde, L. ii. 41/181, *pr. p.* sitting.
Syȝte, L. iii. 36/217, *v. pt. t.* sighed.

Tablere, L. i. 65/989, *s.* the game of tables, or backgammon.
Tac, V. 30/70; Tak, L. ii. 30/70, *v. imp.* take.
Takyne, C. 39/156, *v.* betake.
Tar, L. iii. 30/146; T. 30/146, *v. pt. t.* tore.
Tarsus, St. Alexius sets sail for, 46.
Tauȝtte, L. i. 29/211, *v. pt. t.* taught, instructed. A.S. *tæcan*.
Tee, 16/162, *v.* go, turn, be drawn. A.S. *teon*.
Teiȝ, T. 63/436; Teyȝ, L. iii. 63/436, *v. pt. t.* came, issued. A.S. *teon*.
Teiȝ, T. 64/449; Tey, L. iii. 64/449, *v. pt. t.* drew.
Tene, L. iii. 26/86; T. 26/86; Teone, L. iii. 40/264, *s.* trouble, misery.
Teo, L. iii. 43/274; T. 43/274, *v.* draw, lead. A.S. *teon*.
Tere, L. iii. 52/326, *v. pt. t.* tore.
Teres, L. iii. 28/122, *s. pl.* tears.
Thak, C. 35/122; Thake, C. 49/242, *v.* take. A.S. *tacan*.
Theode, L. iii. 39/258, *s.* land, people.
Therforne, C. 24/40, *adv.* for that, for it.
Thewe, L. iii. 20/2, *adj.* bond, slaves. A.S. *þeow*.
They, L. iii. 25/55; Yþeȝ, T. 25/55, *v. pt. t.* throve, grew.
Thow, C. 62/309, *adv.* there.

Thralle, L. iii. 39/252, *s.* servants. A.S. *þræl*.
Throofe, C. 25/44, *v. pt. t.* throve, grew. O. Icel. *þrifa*.
Tides, L. 19/30, *s. pl.* seasons. A.S. *tid*.
Tit, V. 62/410; Tyd, L. ii. 62/410, *adv.* quickly; as tit = as quickly as possible.
Tiþande, V. 63/417, *s.* tidings.
Tiwes-niȝtte, 12/43, *s.* Tuesday night.
To-breke, L. iii. 36/214, *v.* break in pieces, burst.
To-cleued, L. i. 48/622, *pp.* cut to pieces.
To foren, L. iii. 65/461; To forne, 94/65, *prep.* before.
Tome, L. i. 45/540, *adj.* empty.
Ton, T. 51/317; Tone, L. iii. 51/317, *s. pl.* feet, toes.
Tong, L. iii. 74/560; Tonge, T. 74/560, *s.* a tongue.
Took, L. i. 20/51, *v. pt. t.* betook, gave up.
Toȝt, T. 28/116, *adj.* (?) 'tight little lassie,' natty, well put together.
To-sprynge, L. i. 60/1020, *s.* burst, break.
To-tore, L. i. 43/490, *adj.* with clothes torn into rags, in tattered clothes.
Tourne, L. i. 35/343, *s.* turn, departure.
Tre, L. ii. 37/129; Treo, V. 37/129, *s.* tree.
Tresore, L. i. 76/1119, *s.* treasure, money.
Trine, L. iii. 63/429, *v.* (?) weep.
Trowyd, C. 62/303, *v. pt. t.* believd.
Tueie, 87/186, *adv.* twice.
Tueie, 90/289; Tweie, 12/24, *num. adj.* two. A.S. *twegen*.
Turtel, L. iii. 31/164; Turtle, L. ii. 37/129; Turtul, V. 37/129, *s.* turtle-dove. Lat. *turtur*.
Twyes, L. i. 59/863, *adv.* twice.
Tydingge, L. ii. 63/417, *s.* tidings, news.
Tyght, L. iii. 45/284, *v. pp. t.* intended.

INDEX OF WORDS AND SUBJECTS. 119

Tynt, L. i. 69/1049, *pp.* lost. O. Icel. *tyna*.

Tyt, L. iii. 30/155; T. 30/155, *adv.* soon, quickly.

Þapostles, L. i. 19/19, *s. pl.* the Apostles.

Þapostoile, L. i. 64/967, the apostle.

Þe, L. iii. 52/325, *pro.* those.

Þede, L. ii. 21/11; Þeode, V. 21/11, *s.* country, people. A.S. Þ*eod.*

Þeiȝ, 16/156, *conj.* although, though.

Þeos, V. 63/426, *pr.* these.

Þerwhile, 83/41, *adv.* while.

Þider, L. iii. 33/202; Þuder, T. 33/202, *adv.* thither.

Þilk, 12/20; *pr.* that, those.

Þinketh, L. i. 19/35, *impers. v.* seems, appears. Þhuȝte, V. 20/5, *pt. t.* it seemd.

Þo, L. iii. 24/52; T. 24/52, *adv.* when.

Þole, L. iii. 26/80; Þolye, T. 26/80, *v.* suffer, endure. Þoled, 11/18, *pt. t.* sufferd, endurd. A.S. Þ*olian.*

Þolemod, L. ii. 53/316, *adj.* meek, long-suffering.

Þolemodenesse, 16/157, *s.* patience, meekness.

Þonder, L. i. 46/561, *s.* thunder.

Þonked, L. iii. 23/35; Þonkede, T. 23/35, *v. pt. t.* thanked.

Þoo, L. i. 23/117, *pr.* those.

Þorgh, T. 21/14; Þoruhg, L. iii. 21/14, *prep.* through, throughout.

Þorne, 86/164, *s.* bush, thorn.

Þorst, L. i. 33/281, *s.* thirst.

Þouȝth, 13/55, *v. pt. t.* it seemd.

Þre, L. ii. 21/14; Þreo, V. 21/14, *num. adj.* three. A.S. Þ*reo.*

Þrid, 13/67, *num. adj.* third.

Þrong, L. i. 75/1115, *s.* the crowd.

Þrowe, L. i. 33/285, *s.* time.

Vchadel, V. 55/334, *adv.* every bit, entirely.

Vche, L. i. 21/71, *adj.* each, every.

Veiȝe, T. 73/555, *adj.* dead. A.S. *fǣge.*

Vijs, L. i. 27/171, *s.* face, countenance.

Vnbuxum, 82/16, *adj.* disobedient. A.S. *buhsom* = obedient; '*boxome*, obedient.'—Palsgrave.

Vncouþ, 83/55, *adj.* strange, unknown. A.S. *uncud̄*, unknown, *cud̄*, known.

Vnderfonge, T. 24/44, *v.* take, receive. See Afong.

Vndergo, 15/134, *v. imp.* receive, take.

Vndernam, L. i. 61/914, *v. pt. t.* questiond, examind, understood, perceivd. A.S. *vnderniman*, to undertake.

Vndernom, L. iii. 33/199, *v. pt. t.* understood.

Vndernyme, 84/73, *v. imper.* take in hand, reprove, rebuke.

Vnderstonde, 98/37, *v.* mean, point to.

Vnderȝat, 97/37, *v. pt. t.* perceivd, discoverd. A.S. *undergitan.*

Vnderȝete, 97/41, *v.* discover, determine.

Vndytt, lete hem (lions), 89/254, causd 'em to be removd, shut up. The reverse of *dihtan*, make ready, prepare.

Vnlede, T. 53/333, *adj.* wicked, base. See Halliwell, *s.v.* Vnleed.

Vnmylde, 84/63, *adj.* rude.

Vnneiled, 14/95, *v. pt. t.* unnailed, freed.

Vnneþe, 92/5, *adv.* scarcely. A.S. *uneað* = uneasy; from *eað* = easy.

Vnride, V. 73/542; Vnruyde, L. ii. 73/542, *adj.* excessive.

Vnwrast, L. i. 53/738, *adj.* wicked, base, mean.

Vnwreiȝ, T. 63/434; Vnwrey, L. iii. 63/434, *v. pt. t.* uncoverd. A.S. *unwrigan.*

Vryne, 70/1059, *s.* urine.

Vuel, V. 61/402, *adj.* evil, wicked.

Vyage, C. 30/100, *s.* journey. Fr. *viage.* Lat. *viaticum.*

Vyde, C. 40/161, *adv.* wide.

Vye, L. i. 78/1147, *s.* life. Fr. *vie.*

Wade, L. i. 46/548, *v.* go, pass. A.S. *wadan.* Lat. *vadere.*

Wake, L. i. 19/48, *v.* watch.
War, L. iii. 69/505, *v. imper.* take care, give way.
Ware, L. i. 26/145, *adj.* aware.
Warisshed, L. i. 35/320, *pp.* well protected, saved. Fr. '*Guarir*. To heale, cure, mend, recouer, make whole, restore vnto health.'—Cotgrave.
Waster, L. ii. 21/12, was there.
Waten, L. i. 28/191, *v. pt. t.* went.
Weddowe, C. 73/384, *s.* a widow. A.S. *widewe*.
Wei, V. 33/98; Weie, 85/99, *s.* way, course. A.S. *weg*. O. Fris. *wei*.
Weila-wey, V. 36/125; Weylawey, L. ii. 36/125, wellaway! alas! A.S. *wá la wá = woe, la! woe*.
Wel, 92/4, *adv.* much.
Welde, L. i. 40/431, *v.* to rule, possess.
Wele, L. i. 19/23; Well, C. 21/9, *s.* fortune, wealth. A.S. *wela, weola*.
Wellde, C. 26/54, *v.* manage his affairs. A.S. *weldan*.
Welonye, C. 52/256, *s.* ill-treatment.
Wem, V. 29/65; L. ii. 29/65, *s.* stain, guilt. A.S. *wamm*. Goth. *vamm*.
Wene, 85/122, *v. pr. t.* do ye think. A.S. *wenan*.
Wepþ, L. ii. 37/127, *v. pt. t.* weeps.
Werche, T. 38/246; Wirche, L. iii. 38/246, *v.* work, do, fulfil.
Wernage, C. 27'76, vernage, a kind of white wine.
Werne, L. iii. 70/516, *v.* prevent, stop. A.S. *wernan*.
Werned, C. 22/18, were forbidden, warned from. A.S. *wernan*, to deny, refuse.
Werst, 85/100, *adj.* worst. A.S. *wyrst*.
Wessch, L. ii. 52/311, *v. pt. t.* washt.
West, C. 37/140, *v. pt. t.* knew, wist.
Weste, T. 53/335, *v. pt. t.* wisht.
Wete, V. 70/503, *adj.* wet.
Wetten, C. 63/323, *v.* know. A.S. *witan*.
Wex, L. i. 25/136; C. 25/44, *v. pt. t.* grew, increast.
Whulche, V. 43/207, *pr.* which.

Widewe. L. i. 72/1074, *s.* widow. A.S. *widewe*.
Wijf, L. i. 26/150; Wyf, V. 26/51; Wyffe, C. 26/55, *s.* a wife.
Wikke, L. iii. 61/409, *adj.* wicked, wretched.
Wilk, L. ii. 43/207, *pr.* which.
Willen, L. i. 19/28, *v.* will, wish to.
Wilne, 82/27, *v.* wish. A.S. *wilnian*.
Winne, V. 62/414; Wynne, L. ii. 62/414, *v.* obtain.
Wisse, 97/21, 29, *inf.* teach, guide.
Wissed, L. iii. 24/53; Wissede, T. 24/53, *v. pt. t.* taught. A.S. *wisian*.
Wisselich, 15/133, *adv.* certainly, surely.
Wit, V. 75/566; Wyth, L. ii. 75/566, *s.* senses.
Wite, 83/42, *v. imp.* (?) A.S. *witan*, punish, blame, reproach; not *witan*, wit, know.
Wite, 14/120, *v.* know, be informd. A.S. *witan*.
Witerli, V. 42/196; Wyterly, L. ii. 42/196, *adv.* assuredly.
Witty, L. iii. 27/98; T. 27/98, *adj.* sensible.
Wiþerward, 12/20, *adj.* adverse, opposed. A.S. *wiðerweard*.
Wiþerwynes, 13/85, *s. pl.* enemies, adversaries. A.S. *wiðerwynna*, an enemy.
Wiþseie, 82/19, *v. imp.* oppose.
Wiʒtte, L. i. 31/240, *s.* creature. A.S. *wiʒt*.
Woed, L. iii. 71/531, *adj.* mad.
Won, V. 47/247, *s.* dwelling, place to live in.
Wond, L. iii. 70/515, *v.* cease.
Wondes, L. ii. 50/283, *s. pl.* wounds.
Wone, 13/62, *s.* custom, habit. A.S. [ge]-*wuna*.
Woned, L. iii. 40/259; Y-woned, T. 40/259, *pp.* dwelt, lived.
Wonen, L. i. 19/33, *v.* dwell, live. A.S. *wunian*.

Wonyynge, L. i. 79/1149, pr. p. dwelling.

Woo, L. i. 44/511, adj. sorrowful, mournful.

Wood, L. i. 47/593, adj. furious.

Woodnesse, V. 68/474; Wodnesse, L. ii. 68/474, s. madness.

Wook, L. i. 20/57, v. pt. t.

Wop, 13/64, v. pt. t. beat hard.

Worschiplich, L. i. 20/58, adv. honourably, in honour.

Worþ, 94/33, v. pr. t. is. A.S. weorðan.

Worþe, 83/47, v. shall be.

Worþing-niʒth, 14/87, s. (?)

Wosschen, V. 52/311, v. pt. t. washt.

Wott, C. 26/61, v. pr. t. know, am sure.

Wouʒ, 90/284, s. wall (to fight with his back to), the protection or advantage of his learning.

Wowe, L. iii. 54/346, s. wall. A.S. wag, wæg.

Wrake, L. i. 19/45, s. injury, hurt.

Wrast, C. 63/315, v. wrest.

Wraþþi, L. i. 29/202, v. grieve, vex.

Wrecche, 85/122, s. wretched fool. A.S. wræcce; exul, profugus, miser. Cf. Fr. un misérable.

Wreche, L. i. 29/216, s. ruin, punishment.

Wrie, 84/80, s. betray, disclose.

Wuste, V. 54/326, v. pt. t. knew, was conscious.

Wyghe, C. 73/383.

Wynnying, L. i. 73/1088, s. pleasure, enjoyment.

Wyntersende, C. 54/261, s. winter's end.

Wyntren, 92/22, s. pl. winters, years.

Wytt, C. 25/47, s. sense, understanding.

Wyue, 96/10, s. wife.

Yaffe, C. 31/103, v. pt. t. gave.

Yate, C. 22/18, s. gate, door. A.S. geat.

Ychaunged, L. i. 36/358, pp. changed, altered.

Ycloþed, 15/140, pp. clothed, dresst. A.S. claðian.

Ydytte, 89/242, pp. prepared, ready, A.S. dihtan.

Yfalt, L. i. 61/932, pp. folded.

Yfere, L. i. 60/881, adv. together. A.S. gefera.

Yheled, 84/77, pp. conceald, hidden. A.S. hilan.

Yhent, 95/96, v. catch.

Yheried, 94/64, pp. praisd, glorified.

Yhote, 86/156, pp. named. A.S. hatan.

Yhud, T. 61/409, pp. hidden, conceald.

Ykud, T. 61/410, pp. known, recognisd.

Ykyd, 84/78, pp. shown, made manifest. A.S. cuð.

Ylad, 88/211, pp. taken, led.

Ylast, 93/32, v. lasts, continues.

Yleide, L. i. 64/962, pp. laid.

Ylome, L. i. 21/69, adv. often, frequently. A.S. gelome.

Ylore, L. i. 68/1039, pp. lost.

Ynche, 95/79, s. inch. Lat. uncia.

-ynd, ryming with -ing; sekynd, tyding, L. ii. 39/145.

-yng, for -en. pp.; forsakyng, forsaken, ryming with inf. takyne, betake, C. 39/156.

Ynke, C. 55/265, s. ink.

Ynouh, L. iii. 21/10; Y-nouʒ. T. 21/10, adv. enough. A.S. genoh.

Ypocrite, L. i. 53/739, s. hypocrite.

Yrne, 11/8, s. iron. A.S. iren.

Yse, 84/76, v. see, perceive.

Ysed, 87/175, pp. told, reported.

Yshadewed, L. i. 73/1082, pp. darkend.

Yshred, L. i. 21/82, pp. clad, dresst.

Ysome, 94/20, adj. peaceable, loving. A.S. gesome.

Ysowe, L. i. 61/915, v. saw.

Yswowen, L. i. 17/386, in a swoon.

Yuel, 15/150, adj. evil, ill.

Y-wis, T. 26/78, adv. assuredly, certainly. A.S. gewiss.

Y-wissed, L. iii. 62/426, *pp.* told, informd.
Ywite, L. i. 56/809, *v.* know, find.
Ywonden, 13/57, *pp.* wrapt. A.S. *windan.*
Ywrouȝth, L. i. 25/140, *pp.* wrought, done.
ȝaf, V. 33/93, *v. pt. t.* gave. A.S. *gifan.*
ȝare, L. i. 46/543, *v.* go. A.S. *gearvian.*
ȝare, L. ii. 32/84, *adj.* ready. A.S. *gearu.*
ȝare, V. 43/211, *adv.* readily, quickly.
ȝeden, L. i. 22/85, *v. pt. t.* went, travelled. A.S. *eode* = went.
ȝelde, 88/230, *v.* pay.
ȝer, L. iii. 25/58; ȝere, T. 25/58, *s.* year.
ȝerd, V. 52/302, *s.* court, house. "Yard, or yerd, *hortus.*"—Prompt. Parv.
ȝerne, L. iii. 23/35; T. 23/35, *adv.* earnestly. A.S. *geornian,* to desire.
ȝernend, 93/45, *adv.* eagerly.
ȝeue, L. iii. 25/69; T. 25/69, *v.* to give, graunt.
ȝing, V. 30/68; L. ii. 30/68, *adj.* young. A.S. *geong.*
ȝungge, L. ii. 52/307, *adj.* young.
ȝutt, 82/6, *adv.* yet.

The manufacturer's authorised representative in the EU for product safety is
Oxford University Press España S.A. of el Parque Empresarial San Fernando de
Henares, Avenida de Castilla, 2 – 28830 Madrid (www.oup.es/en or product.
safety@oup.com). OUP España S.A. also acts as importer into Spain of products
made by the manufacturer.

www.ingramcontent.com/pod-product-compliance
Ingram Content Group UK Ltd.
Pitfield, Milton Keynes, MK11 3LW, UK
UKHW022132220326
469240UK00006B/14